D0765795

DOWN
THE
RIVER

A Frame Squad working at Lithgow's in the 1930s

CONTENTS

Foreword	7
Introduction	8
Tom Allison	15
Sammy Barr	17
David Boyd	19
Hugh Boyd	21
Joe Brown	23
Frank Carrigan	25
Pat Clark	27
Willie Clydesdale	29
Paddy Collins	31
Joe Craig	33
Stuart Crawford	35
Lynn Davidones	37
Alex Dickie	39
Bob Dickie	41
Isabel Dickie	43
Isabel Dickie	45
John Dodds	47
John Dollan	49
Sir Robert Easton	51
Hugh Hagan	53
Hugh Hagan (senior)	55
Paul Hagan	57
Nan Hanlon	59
John Innes	61
Margaret Jeffray	63
Tom Jenkins	65
George Kerr	67
Charlie McIntyre	69
Tom McKendrick	71
Colin McKenzie	73
Roddy McKenzie	75
Andrew McLaughlin	77
John McLean	79
Duncan McNeil MSP	81
Willie Miller	83
Tony Mitchell	85
Willie Motherwell	87
George O'Hara	89
Joe O'Rourke	91
John Quigley	93
Fred Reid	95
Jimmy Reid	97
Willie Robb	99
Bill Scott	101
Davy Smart	103
Sandy Stephen	105
Ian Sutherland	107
James Sutherland	109
Alex Wilson	111
Jan Wilson	113
Duncan Winning OBE	115
Sir Eric Yarrow	117
Collapse	119

The Cunard liner Aquitania *on the stocks at John Brown's in 1913*

13

FOREWORD

In October 1997, Ian Jack, editor of Granta magazine, asked us if we could interview people who worked on the building of *QE2* for an article he hoped to prepare. The subsequent article 'Scotland's Last Great Artefact' appeared in Granta 61 and was later reprinted in the Guardian in March 1998. It readily occurred to us that while this article was a tribute to Clydeside's shipbuilding industry through the *QE2*, a broader look at the industry through the eyes of those who worked in it was justified. This became all the more important when it was considered that live connection with this industry, in the way that it once dominated Clydeside, will be severed within a few decades. The rationale for writing this book therefore was to accept that although shipbuilding has barely survived on Clydeside, the completeness with which it once infiltrated every aspect of the river and its people has gone for ever.

Hundreds of thousands of people worked in the shipbuilding industry through the numerous triumphs and depressions that characterised its operational style. For more than a century shipbuilding had been an unavoidable if not unalterable condition of life. On Clydeside, the very first of these people started to trickle through unknown yard gates in the 1840s. At its peak, in the early years of the twentieth century, 100,000 were employed in the shipbuilding and marine engineering industries at any one time.

As generation followed generation into an industry which had become ingrained in the local culture, there was a belief that despite the hardship imposed by often vicious trade cycles, the industry would always be there. Evidence of commercial decline can be traced to the last years of the nineteenth century when other nations joined the industrial elite and offered serious competition for the first time. The twentieth century added its own cocktail of hardship including the worst economic recession in recorded history bracketed by two world wars. Paradoxically, these events added new depth to the hardship associated with shipbuilding as well as underlining its pivotal role during times of national emergency.

Under intense international competition, by the late 1950s Britain had been eclipsed as the world's first shipbuilder. Closures began in the early 1960s while liquidations and rescue attempts seared across national headlines during the 70s and 80s. Contraction was astonishingly rapid to the point where the British shipbuilding industry ceased to be of statistical relevance by the late 1980s.

The group of men and women who would necessarily form the subject of this book are the tail end of this vast labour continuum. The collective memory, aspirations and attitudes of their parents and their grandparents live on with them. It seems only appropriate that they should be respectfully debriefed as an acknowledgement of their role and that of their forebears in this once great industry. To that extent, we have tried to catch the last whispers from the industrial era.

Efforts were made to locate persons who had worked in yards and engine works from Glasgow to Greenock and beyond. The interviews were conducted from the summer of 1999 to the summer of 2000. At this time, four yards remained on Clydeside representing a tenfold reduction in the industry from its heyday. Of these yards, Ferguson at Port Glasgow and BAe Systems at Scotstoun (formerly Yarrow) were well employed. BAe Systems at Govan, formerly Fairfield and most recently known as Kværner Govan, was subjected to an agonising wait to find out if it had any future at all. The small Ailsa yard at Troon, announced its closure in September 2000 despite a healthy order book.

To provide some context, we have described how shipbuilding came to be such a dominating feature of life on Clydeside and how, during the 1960s and 70s, it came to such a rapid demise.

Ian Johnston and Lewis Johnman
June 2001

INTRODUCTION

The origins and growth of shipbuilding and marine engineering on Clydeside is a story of vision and imagination. That such an industry was able to gain a foothold on an unlikely river and grow to a position of leadership says much about attitudes and abilities on Clydeside at the beginning of the nineteenth century. In simple terms, the preconditions for the industry were innovators, entrepreneurs, skilled labour, raw materials and a ready market. The new technology on which this new industry would sit was steam power. It was the builders of these steam engines and not traditional wooden shipbuilders who recognised the potential which steam propulsion promised. They foresaw that ships built of iron rather than wood offered a better platform for steam engines.

Finding a practical means to employ the steam engine to propel a boat forwards began to preoccupy several people in the last decades of the eighteenth century. In this, Scotland was to play an important role. As early as 1788, William Symington and Patrick Miller between them managed to propel a 25 feet long craft at the speed of five miles per hour. It was not until March 1802 however, that Symington, commissioned by Lord Dundas, built the *Charlotte Dundas* to tow barges on the Forth & Clyde Canal. Described as the first practical steamboat, this vessel was able to tow two seventy-ton barges a distance of over nineteen miles in six hours. In the United States, Robert Fulton started what is considered to be the first commercially successful steamboat service in the year 1807 on the River Hudson. The first comparable service in Europe was on the Clyde in 1812 when Henry Bell, proprietor of the Helensburgh Baths, started operating the twenty five-ton *Comet*. The engine for this little craft was built in Glasgow by John Robertson.

By 1816, there were twenty steamboats plying the Clyde. All these wooden craft were built in the lower reaches of the river while all the engines except two, which were a product of Boulton Watt & Co in Birmingham, were constructed in Glasgow. As the steam engine began to find favour as a reliable alternative to the vagaries of wind and tide, technical improvements to the engine were made. These improvements were concerned with greater mechanical efficiency and improved fuel economy.

In the long period of wood and sail that preceded steam and iron, Glasgow had no marine industries of any consequence. Dumbarton, Port Glasgow and Greenock however, had a number of wood building yards, among them Scott's which first started business in 1711. Also, Glasgow had no conceivable future to offer any maritime industry because the river was woefully inadequate. The upper reaches of the Clyde resembled little more than a shallow but wide stream with numerous sandbanks and obstructions along its length. The Clyde had to be made navigable and Glasgow accessible to ocean-going ships. Through a series of Acts of Parliament starting in 1770, the River Clyde, until then only fifteen inches deep in places at low water, was deepened to seven feet. Successive Acts deepened the river to nine feet (1809), thirteen feet (1825), and seventeen feet (1840).

Over a period of many years the Clyde was progressively straightened and deepened to allow large vessels to sail into Glasgow Harbour. The first shipbuilder of any account to take advantage of improving conditions on the upper reaches, Robert Barclay, established a small yard for building wooden vessels in 1818 at Stobcross. By 1842, three others had joined Barclay within the city boundaries, Tod & Macgregor, Thomas Wingate and Robert Napier. What distinguished the last three shipbuilders was the adoption of iron instead of wood from the outset. In 1845 Barclay was joined by Robert Curle and in 1847 they too commenced shipbuilding in iron.

Of all the shipbuilders so far mentioned the most important

The foundry at John Brown's in the 1900s

was Robert Napier, a brilliant engineer who together with his cousin David Napier laid the foundations of marine engineering and shipbuilding on Clydeside. Robert Napier was no mean businessman and it was he who enabled Samuel Cunard to set up the steamship line later known as the Cunard line. Napier also designed and built the engines for Cunard's first Atlantic steamers, the hulls of which were built by Robert Duncan at Greenock. Clydeside's link with Cunard endured until 1968 with the completion of the *QE2* at Clydebank. Napier's other great contribution to the development of the shipbuilding industry was to train the next generation of marine engineers and shipbuilders. These included John Elder who went on to establish his works at Fairfield and James and George Thomson who founded the company later taken over by John Brown & Co.

The continuing development of marine steam technology through compound and later triple expansion machinery ensured that Clydeside maintained the lead in innovation. The new engines were more fuel efficient, reducing the cost of sea transportation. By the 1870s, Clydeside had become the leading shipbuilding and marine engineering centre in the world with a track record of excellence. The express transatlantic liner became a specialism and much of Clydeside's reputation stems from the quality of workmanship associated with these vessels. Winning the Blue Riband for the fastest crossing on the prestigious North Atlantic route became a purely Clydeside affair with the Clydebank and Fairfield yards the main contenders.

By the end of the 1880s, the population of Glasgow had expanded to over 770,000. By this time there were forty three shipyards in the Clyde district including one at Rutherglen, one each on the Monkland and Forth & Clyde canals and four on the River Cart at Paisley. Many of the yards that would survive into the twentieth century were by then flourishing. Perhaps best known on the upper reaches was John Elder's Govan yard which, in 1889, had been renamed the Fairfield Shipbuilding & Engineering Co. At Clydebank, J&G Thomson's yard had been acquired by Sheffield forgemasters and armour manufacturers John Brown & Co in 1899 and was set to build some of the largest and best known ships in the world.

Statistically, the growth in this industry had been dramatic. In 1812, two steam ships totalling 55 tons were built on the Clyde. By 1853 the number of ships launched was 86, totalling 61,044 tons. Of these 79 were built of iron. By 1895, 360,152 tons of shipping was launched on the Clyde amounting to 31.2% of the UK total and 27.6% of the world total. In other words, in 1895 the UK built 88% of all the world's ships with over a one in four chance of a ship being Clyde built. The peak year of output for Clyde shipbuilding was 1913 when 756,976 tons were produced. In the same year, ships' machinery totalling 1,111,440 horse power was constructed in the engine shops. Despite the great rise in output since 1895, the Clyde percentage of the world's ships had nevertheless slipped to just under 18%. This activity masked the fact that other nations, France, Italy, Holland, Germany, Japan and the USA, were constructing ships for themselves.

By the end of the nineteenth century, Clydeside took a leading role in warship building in response to the worldwide responsibilities of the Royal Navy. In October 1900 the Glasgow Herald was able to claim that 'the position of the Clyde as the premier shipbuilding river in the world is once more beyond question for on its banks are being built more warships than are being built anywhere.'

With a dominant position in building merchant tonnage, naval tonnage became of increasing importance. In the face of Admiralty prejudice which favoured the Royal Dockards and private builders on the Thames, the first naval contracts were secured by Napier in the 1840s. As Clydeside developed, Elder at Fairfield, Thomson at Clydebank, Scott's at Greenock and Beardmore at Dalmuir were successful in winning orders for all classes of warships up to and including battleships.

The first to build a large yard was John Elder in 1860 at Govan. Next came J&G Thomson at Clydebank. Biggest of all the Clydeside shipyards was William Beardmore's Naval Construction Works at Dalmuir. Built between 1901 and 1906, this yard was expressly intended for the construction of large warships and passenger vessels. Between them, the three large Clydeside yards employed over 30,000 people.

The Ship Drawing Office at Alexander Stephen's in the 1940s

Even after Beardmore opened his new yard, the expansion of shipbuilding was not over. In 1907, Yarrow & Co moved their specialist warship yard from Poplar on the Thames to Scotstoun. Labour rates on the Thames were high but with its skilled labour pool and multitude of sub-contractors and suppliers, the Clyde was a far more appropriate place to be located. The same logic applied to Belfast shipbuilders Harland & Wolff. In 1912, they bought over three old yards at Govan including Napier's and built a large modern yard which opened on the eve of World War I. The last new shipyard to locate on Clydeside was the Blythswood, built on a greenfield site at Scotstoun in 1919.

At Port Glasgow and Greenock there were a large number of smaller yards generally concentrating on the construction of standard cargo ships. The name of Lithgow, which would later have considerable influence on shipbuilding, first appeared in 1918 when William Lithgow took over Russel & Co at Port Glasgow. Over time, Lithgow would acquire an interest in many shipyards and establish the largest shipbuilding group in the world.

By the end of World War I, the industry had reached its maximum physical extent on the Clyde. Many of the original pioneering companies had either disappeared or been incorporated into successor businesses.

The result was a river dotted with heavily industrialised towns – Greenock, Port Glasgow, Dumbarton, Old Kilpatrick, Dalmuir, Clydebank, Paisley and Glasgow. Machine shops, platers' sheds, engine works, structural engineering works, boiler shops, foundries, steel works and locomotive works filled the landscape. Hundreds of chimneys pushed their sooty deposits into the atmosphere through day and night. The industrial landscape that emerged was a closed environment of tenements, works and churches often pressed hard against one another.

The influx of large numbers of people into the new industries, prompted the organisation of labour to fight for improvements in working conditions. Employers became organised in the form of the Employers Federation and thus both sides of what would prove to be a fractious relationship sought to control the industry. When work was in abundance, unions exerted pressure on employers including strike action to increase wages and shorten the working week. When orders were few, employers reduced wages and lengthened working hours using the tactic of the 'lockout'. Conflict became in-grained and memories long. Bitter struggles were difficult to forget. Lack of trust permeated the industry long after such tribal behaviour should have been abandoned.

Perhaps best known of the labour organisations was the Boilermakers. Named after the activity which was central to the steam era, making iron boilers to generate steam, the Boiler-makers commanded the new skills required to take this reluctant metal and form, bend and punch it into shape. From the outset, boilermakers were sectionalised and thus drillers, platers, caulkers and riveters came into existence as separate trades under the general title of boilermakers.

Nevertheless, in all its constituent parts, a great industry had been created whose products could be seen and admired in every corner of the globe. For those involved it had become an all-pervasive way of life, reaching into almost every household, creating an economy precariously focused on making just one product: ships.

The vulnerability of the industry had not gone unnoticed. After the grim experience of the 1930s depression, Governments tried to broaden the manufacturing base of the West of Scotland as a hedge against the collapse of heavy industry. As late as 1952, however, Charles Oakly, editor of *Scottish Industry*, was able to say that 250,000 people worked in these industries. With twenty two shipyards still in existence between Glasgow and Troon, shipbuilding and marine engineering alone accounted for about one third of that total.

Although no-one could have foreseen events to come, the conditions had been created for the rout of an industry.

Crane driver Jackie Devins working over Ship 813 at Govan Shipbuilders in 1987

Tom Allison
Draughtsman, Barclay Curle & Co Ltd

I started in A&J Inglis at Pointhouse as an office boy with a view to going into the drawing office. At that time in the 50s, whale-catchers were the big thing and we were churning them out. I was only there about a year, but while I was there I did everything. I was the office boy, I was chief cook and bottle washer, I was the ambulanceman, I was the gateman. I was also rat-catcher. I set traps in the office block and when I went in on Monday morning I had to clear up the mess. It was unbelievable. Inglis was a great wee shipyard.

In 1950 I went to Barclay Curle to start my apprenticeship. My father was a shipwright in Barclay Curle's. When I did my time in that yard, you did six months of your apprenticeship in the shipyard, and when I went to the shipwrights' department, I got my father's check number. Obviously somebody had remembered. Barclay's were really busy of course. The first ship I worked on was the *Uganda* and then other big British India cargo liners.

The system was that the next job on the list was yours. In the steel section which I was in, we had wee Jimmy Murphy, who was an absolute terror but a great man to work for, you'd do anything for him. He'd lost a foot in the First World War and you could hear him coming, the thump thump of his foot. He saw every journeyman once a day and the apprentices twice a day. Unless it was a job that was top of the priority list, he would virtually live with you. He really was a first class man. An absolute terror, but everyone thought the world of him. But if the next job on wee Jimmy's list was yours, no matter what it was, how complicated it was, you got it and he steered you. The worst thing you could do if you came to a particular result was to tell Jimmy you copied it off a previous job. You were expected to think. The training there was really first class, there was no such thing as a boy's job. In John Brown's, where I worked later, there were boys' jobs. I couldn't understand how you were going to learn if you were stuck with the so-called simple jobs.

I went to Connel's drawing office for one year and then on to John Brown's. You got some respect. Instead of just being Jimmy or Willie, you were now Mr Allison. I can remember in John Brown's there were guys there who were in their 50s, early 60s, and they'd been there all their days, they were still Willie and Jimmy, boys who'd served their time there. So they were definitely not regarded with the same respect as those of us who'd come in as new starts.

The big contract at the time in Brown's was the *QE2*. The conditions you worked in were appalling. There was a building just down the road from the drawing office called the horse trough, and that's exactly what the offices were like. Appalling place. The managers and foremen worked in these horrible buildings. Underfoot conditions outside in the yard were appalling, you walked through mud to get to the berths. I was given the title Assistant Manager, which immediately got me in the bad books of the people I was going to be working most closely with, the Manager's Assistants. It's a subtle play on words, but it was very important to them.

On the ship, I had three or four areas that I was responsible for. While I would be away looking after one area, the team of electricians, plumbers, joiners that you had left in another area would disappear because someone had a problem in another area and needed more hands. So your team disappeared, and when you came back everything was just hanging in the air.

Barclay Curle's were quite successful as they started a planning department. Brown's had no planning whatsoever. To my mind no organisation at all, but at the end of the day they got there, which says something about their system. I can't honestly say I liked working on the *QE2* because you were restricted by what the so-called architects were doing. They wanted a chair where the pillar was so the pillar moved, not the chair.

I think it was inevitable that the industry was going to decline. I think lots of things were instigated purely to suit the accountant rather than the engineer or the shipbuilder.

Sammy Barr
Welder, Charles Connell & Co Ltd

When I left the school at the age of fourteen in about 1945 or 1946 I started as a plater's boy first of all. When I was fifteen I started as an apprentice welder. You had the choice of being a riveter, a caulker, a burner or a welder. So I went for the welding game as there weren't many welders in the yard at the time, it was mostly riveters. Both my dad and brother were blacksmiths at Stephen's and according to them there was no future in that, so it was the welding for me. There would only be about forty or so welders in Connell's when I started and there were still some dilutee women in the yard employed as crane drivers and rivet heaters. It was a good yard to work in. Everybody that worked there knew each other and they all lived in the same areas. When my time was out, I went into the army to do national service and when I came back from that in 1954, I went back into Connell's.

Even before the time of the UCS work-in there was a real sense of crisis in the industry. Lots of us knew that British shipowners were ordering abroad in increasing numbers and that if we lost our market then that would be it. We had talks with Wedgwood Benn with the view of advocating the nationalisation of both shipbuilding and shipping but there had been the Geddes Report and there was a Shipbuilding Industry Board and he seemed content with that but nobody really addressed the problem of shipping. Then there was UCS, Connell's, Fairfield's, Stephen's, Yarrow's and John Brown's, the five yards, and that was successful up to 1970 when the government decided to shut the lot down. There was a big reaction from the shop stewards and workers who were determined not to let the yards shut. The response was amazing because sometimes as a shop steward it was difficult to get a reaction from the workforce. The very first demonstration that we had in Glasgow was supported by the churches and school children among others. There were about 50,000 people demonstrating

in our support, and that gave us lots of publicity. The miners sent us money. In fact, money came in from all over Britain and abroad and it was put into a fund run by the shop stewards down in Brown's. After about six weeks we had another demonstration, one of the biggest demonstrations ever seen in Glasgow. Big Jimmy Reid played a magnificent role, he was a great orator. Jimmy Airlie was great as well, a very powerful speaker. So we appointed big Jimmy the Chairman and I was the Convenor in Connell's so I became the third man. Three Terrible Men as we were termed in the papers. We discussed tactics and I suggested that we should have a work-in. We take the yards over and we run them so that nobody goes down the road. It was a totally new tactic in the struggle for the right to work, to saving your job. After that, the government nationalised the industry.

British Shipbuilders was good because you met stewards from all over the country during the wage negotiations which covered all of us rather than previously where it was yard by yard, district by district as well as national. Under BS we got all the wages up to the same level rather than everybody getting different rates for the same job. After all the arguments about BS it was privatised again, Mrs Thatcher was hell bent on closing the industry down. Fairfield's, where I'd gone after Connell's closed, was sold to a Norwegian company, Kværner. I say sold but in reality, Kværner were given money by the government to get rid of the yard. Brown's was on oil related work and on the upper river the only yard that's left is Govan and the future there is uncertain.

I really enjoyed my working life in shipbuilding. I was a man that was a shop steward, a man that was a convenor but I was a man that kept the overalls on. I always found it was better to stay on the job. I retired in 1993 with a wee bit of ill health but I'd done my stint.

David Boyd
Draughtsman, Alexander Stephen & Co Ltd

In 1950 I started in Stephen's shipyard at Linthouse. I wanted to start in the drawing office. They had an exam there, but I was too late to get in, so they said to me to come down and work on one of the ships. So I did that, metal working, and I enjoyed it. I then went into the drawing office, doing outfit drawings, accommodation units and that sort of thing. Eventually, I got to take the exam which was a combination of maths, English and an IQ test. There wasn't really a drawing element to it as such. I then went to night school. The firm didn't actually send you, but there was a strong recommendation that you should go. So I did three years at Glasgow High School, three nights a week. It was home from work, a quick tea and out again and, of course, you'd have your homework to do as well. The night classes were a combination of technical drawing, maths and naval architecture. It was hard going but enjoyable nonetheless.

Stephen's was a good family yard, well run. We always said that we were unfortunate in that we'd closed it down, but it was good training and the working atmosphere was excellent. In terms of the ships, when I went into Stephen's, they were building a lot of ships for the Union Steamship Company of New Zealand. They were just finishing a passenger liner, the *Olympia*, which was launched unnamed because the Queen was launching the *Britannia* on the same day at John Brown's. We were, at the same time, building lots of fruit carriers for Elder's and Fyffes and lots of cargo liners. So the work was very varied all the way from passenger liners, fruit boats that could carry passengers, cargo liners and straightforward cargo boats. There was also naval work. We built a destroyer, *Defender*, and two frigates *Lowestoft* and *Zulu*. There were a lot of differences between the naval side and the merchant work.

I was at Stephen's from 1950 to 1967 but things were getting dodgy well before the creation of Upper Clyde Shipbuilders. It was well known that at least one yard, maybe two, would close

as part and parcel of the deal. I expected the worst. Indeed, I'd told my wife to expect the worst and that we'd all get made redundant. She claims to this day that I told her that in 1967 but even though I'd managed to work on for another thirty years beyond that date, she was still expecting the redundancy money! It was the last day that she ever listened to me.

I was transferred from Stephen's to Fairfield's, which was a very different yard. Sure you did the same sort of job, but strangely, given that this was at the tail end of the Fairfield Experiment, we always felt that the systems we had at Stephen's were much more advanced than at Fairfield's. For example, a small point, they still filed information in old-fashioned wooden drawers whereas we had metal filing cabinets and we brought a whole pile of those along with us. So I went through Stephen's, Fairfield's, UCS, and then nationalisation. Although these events seemed at the time to be points of crisis, what I was actually doing didn't really change that much. I think that was more about the nature of the work than anything else.

The big change was really the introduction of computers to the drawing office. They made a tremendous difference. By that time I was in charge of the office, so the boys all went for retraining and I just had to make sure that the drawings were turned out. It certainly sped things up. Initially it seemed to slow things down, but once the library of things was built up, things really did get quicker. Prior to that you could draw the same thing over and over again. You could get stencils but the scales might not be appropriate, so we'd normally work on a scale of about 1 to 50. We'd do the whole outline of the ship and they would go to the owners and then come back and we'd incorporate any changes. All in all though, I've had a really good working life in shipbuilding and I think it's just a shame to look at the river now and think about all the jobs and work that's gone.

Hugh Boyd
Welder, Lobnitz & Co Ltd

I didn't really have a desire to go into shipbuilding. My father was away in the forces and it was mother that got me down at Whiteinch and it was a case of a job was a job. There was clearly a big push on for welding at the time and it had become a lot more common than a few years before. The earnings in it were good and as you were on constant piecework so you could make really good money so that was the attraction.

I started in 1943 during the war as an office boy in a light engineering and welding company down at Whiteinch. After that I started in the shop where they did repair work, caissons and such like, for war-damaged merchant ships. I worked there for a while and then went down to Lobnitz's yard at Renfrew and served my time there as a welder. During the war we did minesweepers, corvettes and barges. In Lobnitz's during the war, there were some women doing welding as well as women crane drivers, rivet heaters and electricians, all sorts of jobs. When my time was out, I went to the Blythswood yard at Scotstoun, and worked there until about 1957. I went down South for a few months but didn't like that much so I came back and started in Fairfield's, then John Brown's, then down the lower reaches to Scott's and Lithgow's and across the river to Scott's of Bowling. I finished up at Yarrow's. I've been out for eight years now.

I have no regrets at all about going into welding it's been a good job. Mind, it did have its down side which we didn't know at the time but you'd maybe be working in a boiler room or engine room with engineers and you'd come out covered in white dust. Asbestos. They called the guys that worked with asbestos the white mice as they were working with it all the time lagging pipes, all sorts of difficult jobs and they would just be covered in it from head to foot. I remember going for a test for

TB in the yards. There was a big campaign against it, but I don't remember any testing for asbestos.

One of the main differences in the yards was the size. Lobnitz, for example, was a small yard and you'd know just about everybody that worked in it. After the war it reverted to its specialism which was dredgers so you worked on a very narrow range of ships. If you went into say, Brown's, it was huge, a big workforce, good atmosphere though, but the range of ships that you worked on was incredible, liners, ferries, oil tankers, naval work and Fairfield would be much the same. Latterly though, there was a marked decline in liner and ferry work and the mainstays of the job became bulk carriers and tankers. Back in the 50s you never really knew if your job was secure but there were so many yards on the river that you could be out of one and in another in the same day. I wasn't paid off all that often because I did some good long stints in some of the yards. I was in Fairfield's at the time of the Fairfield Experiment when Ian Stewart took over and it was run as a public/private partnership with the government and unions involved. Stewart brought in two other guys, Jim Houston and Oliver Blanford, and there were big changes, consultants, and all the rest of it. Whole bunches of us were taken off to Esher in Surrey for courses in job evaluation, similar to time and motion study, work study. The whole concept seemed to be based on tearing up the rule book and getting some flexibility in. It might have a chance of working but the whole UCS thing derailed it and Stewart and his team were out. But of all the yards I worked in the Blythswood was the best. True it specialised in tankers which are hardly at the fashionable end of the market but the quality of workmanship in there was absolutely fantastic, every ship was a beauty.

Joe Brown
Plumber, John Brown & Co Ltd

I started in 1938, I had no family in shipbuilding but times were hard, it was a job and I wanted to get a trade. It was a five-year apprenticeship then and my original idea was to do two and a half years at John Brown's and then the rest of it at a plumber's in Clydebank where my sister was secretary to the owner. That was all changed by the war though and I was called up in 1942. I worked at Devonport and various places in the South of England, mainly working on landing craft. By the end of the war I was out in Singapore and came back in a mine-sweeper but when we got into the Mediterranean we were ordered to do some sweeping and that delayed my return. I did see Italy in the distance but that was as close as I got!

I got demobbed and I restarted at Brown's in 1946 and one of the first jobs that I worked on was refitting the *Queen Elizabeth*. I really wanted a good technical education and that just wasn't available at John Brown's so I went to night school for about six years and did my City and Guilds, in Clydebank and at Stow College. I would come in from work, get changed, eat, be off to college, come back, bed and then up again for work in the morning. I found it really hard sometimes to be back as an apprentice beside the younger ones. I was older and had been half way around the world during the war. I liked the yard though, it was always a good-humoured place to work. The humour could be pretty black which I suppose was a way of coping with what could be really rough conditions. In the winter, if it was frosty, sometimes the ice would stay on the steel plates for days at a time, you were really out in all the elements.

I worked back and forward between the plumber's shop and the berth so the work was pretty varied. Think of all the different things that pipes have to carry on a ship, all the different lengths, angles, joints and such like that need to be made. For example, on a liner like the *QE2*, there are now what look like really elegant columns all over the public rooms of the ship, but inside there's literally thousands of miles of piping, ducting and so forth carrying all sorts of essential services to all parts of the ship.

You did though, get a sense that things were beginning to slide. Not long after I became a shop steward, the District Committee wrote to the Clyde Shipbuilders Association asking for a meeting about modernisation. Some people had been abroad and had seen what was happening there. But they refused to meet us. I'm sure that this is documented in the Glasgow Herald. It was sometimes the case that a ship would be gone for a year to eighteen months before a final cost was arrived at so there was no idea of profitability. The liner *Kungsholm* had run up a huge loss and there was a feeling that if the *QE2* went wrong then the yard would close.

The level of distrust on both sides of the industry was intense, even things that seem really minor now. For example, take the *QE2*. Although it wasn't the last ship launched from the yard it was pretty late in the day. That was the first launch where workers were invited onto the platform. That seemed so serious at the time, we only built the things after all, that we had to have a stewards' meeting about it to see if we would accept.

I remember the first computer coming into the yard, the thing was the size of a house and it used to calculate the pay. The currency hadn't been decimalised at the time so they had to adjust the wages up and down every week. Everything was fine when they went up but when they went down there was nearly a riot. Trying to explain this as a shop steward was no fun and it kept me home late every other Friday night.

Frank Carrigan
Loftsman, Charles Connell & Co Ltd

I started my time in Connell's in 1965 as an apprentice rigger and spent six months at that. At the time, rigging involved loads of shrouds for masts and derricks. Part of the job was to make up the wires which would attach all of these various things. I was then transferred to the shipwright department and then went into working in the loft, in order to complete my five year apprenticeship. The loft was completely different work and was the linkage between the technical side of the shop floor where the steel was prepared and the drawing office. The architect would send a drawing down to the office and effectively it would be sent to us to round off, to 'sweeten', to shape, and that was our primary function. If you needed say 600 particular shapes we would organise the maximum cut from any given plate so that there would be no wastage.

I wasn't long in the loft when technology started to take over and they introduced a thing called the 'Messer burner'. The loft became like a drawing area where you worked to one-tenth scale and the machine had what was called 'the magic eye', a perspex drawing would be completed to a tenth of the scale and the machine would follow the outline of the drawing. The range of skills within my trade was fantastic – from drawings to the delivery to platers, prefabrication, keel-laying with theodalites etc, all the way through to the launching of the ship.

The layout of yards was different in many ways as was the way in which manning levels were determined. In Connell's, you always had a high proportion of steelworkers. The engines were subcontracted and almost all the finishing trades were subcontracted as well. The engines were built by Kincaid's and the electrical work was done by Robertson's, etc.

There wasn't really a sense of crisis at the time of the Upper Clyde Shipbuilder's work-in, more a sense of determination.

The sense that one had both dignity and a right to work. It wasn't the first time that the idea of 'Clyde built' actually came to mean something, and that was something which, quite rightly, the shop stewards' committee used to its utmost. So there was no real sense of crisis. The huge degree of dignity bestowed upon the shop stewards and the workforce had to be set against people who were talking about an industry which they knew nothing about. There were all these abilities in the shipyard beyond the so called 'metal bashers'. I could go into Connell's and I could get a haircut, play chess with a chessmaster, watch somebody do The Times crossword in ten minutes – you had this range of skills, knowledge. If you wanted to go in for running, fine; if you had a bad back and needed physiotherapy, fine, there would be somebody there or somebody who knew somebody.

I think ultimately the will to support shipbuilding was lost by politicians. We'd called for years for a nationalised industry, but the mere fact that we got it allowed them to bleed us to death. The decision was taken after Griffin and Atkinson, to reduce the industry to a rump and when Graham Day came in he was little more than an axeman. When Thatcher won the election in 1979, I was working in Govan. I was walking down the road with Jimmy Airlie. He said, 'we'll go back fifty years and we'll lose the shipbuilding industry.' Big Airlie's words have come true.

But one image that stays with me is walking in that door at sixteen and getting the fright of my life. The main things had to be the camaraderie the friendship and the crack. I could go in to Connell's on a Monday morning feeling terrible and if I wasn't laughing after ten minutes there was something wrong.

Pat Clark
Welder, Scott Lithgow Ltd

In Greenock you either worked in the yards or the sugar works. I started in shipbuilding on the 21 August 1972 straight from school. At that time you started as what was called a general shipbuilding apprentice. My father was a plater and my grandfather was a 'hauder-on'. Most of my uncles also worked in the yards. My brother is the black sheep of the family, he's a draughtsman! There was a training centre which we went to in the first year and you did a bit of each trade, at least that was the case in the boilermaking trades. At the end of that year I was sent up to Lithgow's to work as they were looking for a couple of boys to serve their time as loftsmen. So I did a year in there, six months in the full-scale loft and six months in the tenth-scale loft. After that I was put out with the platers, to get more experience, but that was the end of it. I was never invited back into the loft! At the time though, Scott Lithgow were starting about four or five hundred apprentices a year, they didn't all finish obviously, but it seems incredible now to think of the numbers.

As an apprentice plater, you were looked after by an apprentice supervisor and there were certain things you had to do while you were serving your time. I was taken in hand by the Head Foreman Plater who tended to look out for boys that he thought were particularly keen. I started with two old timers basically making stools, things like that. Then I went to the main plating shed and worked with the rollerman on the cold frame bender. Now and then you'd get a wee job to do yourself but basically you did a bit of everything. When I finished my time, I was up in the Glen yard, which they called Disneyland because it was full of characters. Again, it was what was called jobbing work, I was basically making all sorts of things that went onto the boat and was there until six months after my time was out. Then the foreman came and took me out onto the boat. We were building supertankers at the time, and the first job I got was to put a flat bar right along the top of the rollover. This was about a hundred feet above the berth and they gave me a harness. The flat bar was eventually going to take the guard rails on the ship's side and I was working to the outside of that. The harness was only a crotch harness though and I thought that if I was to fall I'd probably fall head first in which case I'd come out of the bloody thing. After that, I did quite a lot of marking off and various other jobs but I really enjoyed it, I would never have left the yards.

When the problem with UCS happened earlier, there was no real sense of crisis on the Lower Clyde. The view was that the crowd up the river had all sorts of problems but that we, Scott Lithgow, were all right because we were in the right type of market, supertankers, and we were the only yard in Scotland that could build them. Then there were the two oil price rises and that was the end of that. There were some horrendous decisions made with attempts to get into various things like oil rigs. British Shipbuilders decided that they would specialise in various markets and we were put into the Offshore Division to build rigs. At the time people thought it was great as this seemed to be a growing market. One of the problems however was that being designated an offshore yard meant that we no longer qualified for intervention funding, so getting back into the ship market was going to be well-nigh impossible. Then there was the problem that rig building was totally different and I think that the first rig took a really long time to build. We'd built two drill ships in the early 1970s at the Cartsdyke Yard and apparently they were really good and that might have influenced the decision to put us into the offshore section but rigs were a totally different thing and in the end it busted the yard. But I don't think anyone thought that we'd be sitting here today with hardly a yard left.

Willie Clydesdale
Welder, John Brown & Co Ltd

I started when I was fifteen in 1941. It was nearly all riveting machines then and I used to enjoy watching, the way people worked. They were hard workers. There was a big push on for welders at the time and I went in for that, although very few others did which I found surprising. There seemed to be a view that welding was just a passing phase but to me it seemed as if it was the future. I left the yards when I was eighteen and went into the forces. When I came back, I went into Fairfield's which was an interesting yard in that if you hadn't served your time in it you were treated differently. The foreman knew all of his people and as a consequence, you would get the worst sort of jobs. You found it hard to make a wage there.

When I left Fairfield, I went for a wander. For instance I went to Wales and worked on a steel plant that was being built and when I came back, I went to John Brown's at Clydebank. It was really just a job to tide me over but I got married and that was my wandering days over. Brown's was a different place altogether, there was more of a family feel to it and I felt part of that. I enjoyed working in the shipyard but it was a rough, raw, place.

Winter in the yard was horrible and you always seemed to get jobs above deck and in the summer you'd always be below deck. What kept you from cracking up was the people. There was a bit of antagonism between welders and riveters in the early days because the riveters could see that plates were being joined by a weld rather than three rows of rivets, so they weren't too happy with that situation. But they tended to hold out instead of seeing that welding was eventually going to do away with their jobs. The riveters were really hard-working though, there's no doubt about that. They were on strict piecework and they would just pee or shit where they were working so they didn't have to stop. That was all right outside the boat but if you were working inside, say in a double bottom, where you had to crawl around to do wee bits of welding, your hand would sometimes go splat. There was a wee bloke, a cleaner-up, you'd go to him and the gaffer would give him a line to clean it up. Mind you, he got something like half a crown per shit and I think he used to do half of the shitting himself – made himself a fortune.

I became a shop steward in 1960 and got involved with the national officials and such like. They kept hammering on about what was happening abroad and about the advances that were being made in Germany, Sweden and Japan. They'd been there and seen what was happening. But we tended to turn a deaf ear, the 'boilermaker's ear', and we really held things up by insisting on double manning on a lot of machines that were being brought in. We only looked to the moment and thought we were going to lose jobs and at the end of the day we were too reluctant to move forward. By the 1960s things were beginning to get tighter and every order seemed to get harder and harder. Management seemed very reluctant to face up to the unions, so the management was also to blame in that they could have pushed more things through, and made us face up to events. My greatest feeling is of the guys I met at Brown's and the camaraderie.

When I was at Fairfield's I was late one morning so I had to see the timekeeper. He asked me where I lived and I said, 'Maryhill'. 'So do I', he said. 'How do you get in?' he asked. I said, 'I go down to St George's Cross and catch the tube', and he said, 'So do I. I'm here on time and you're late, so you can go home'. But, Brown's was a different sort of place altogether, it was pretty fair.

Paddy Collins
Shipwright, William Hamilton & Co Ltd

I started work when I was fourteen in a shipbreaking yard called Smith's. I did about six or seven months there and then went into the Clyde shipbuilding yard and started my time as a carpenter. I was in there about four months when it folded and we were sent down to Hamilton's to finish our time. Actually I started as an apprentice shipwright. Shipwrights were most concerned with iron work, but when I went to Hamilton's it was mostly wood-work, decking and such like but it was essentially the same trade. When a boy went into the yard at first you'd be attached to an iron squad, the ship would be built one frame at a time and you'd have squads working on either side of the boat, the job would be to run about the yard collecting bolts, whatever, for the job. So I was with a squad at the Clyde yard but when I went down to Hamilton's I got sent onto the deck as a liner-off which was lining-off the deck hatches, ventilators, basically all the deck fittings. I was with one journeyman for nearly a year and after about five or six months he had taught me how to read the plans so that after about nine months I could do the job myself. After that I was sent out with another guy, a carpenter, and we were working on big ships for Brocklebank's. Large ships for the day with great long boat decks, eighty, ninety feet long. That was all woodwork, five by two and a half Oregon pine. I learnt how to lay decking. I then got sent to work with another old guy to learn how to lay the windlass sole, a nine inch plank about four inches thick which the windlass sat on.

When my time was out we had a ship ready for launch, a molasses boat. The gaffer came up with a great big long list of names and it was a case of you're off, you're off and you're off. He passed me by and at this time I was working with one of the under-gaffer's sons and I said to him that the gaffer had passed me by and he mustn't have seen me. He replied that I'd been seen all right but that I was getting kept on. I didn't leave until 1944 so that would have been about 1933 or 1934.

I was in an iron squad until 1942 when I was made a leading hand. My mate at the time, big Malky MacDonald was anxious to get out as there was more money in ship repairing. So we went to Lamont's where the dock was absolutely full of boats. At that time it would be about £4 for a 48-hour week but you got about 2d an hour extra as a repair worker. If you worked on an oil tanker you got 6d an hour extra if you worked on the deck and 9d an hour extra if you worked on the tanks. Repair had a huge priority and if we were making that sort of money the employers must have been making a packet. I was in fifty-one years in all between shipbuilding and ship repairing and never got a ha'penny for it. I did get one hundred pounds from Lamont's but I wouldn't have got it but for Mick Gillan, the shop steward. I told him I was packing it in and he said that he'd go and see the managing director who told him to come back the following week. I'd been in the place 34 years. If he had paid me off at 60, I would have got twenty weeks wages but after 60 it was progressively reduced until at 65 you got nothing. There was a guy who left about the same time as me, aged 70 and he didn't get a penny. Mind you, Lamont's was a good place to work – the lads were great and everybody helped each other out. The biggest change I saw was the welding. It did away with the riveting squads and a lot of caulking. Sure you still had caulkers but to nothing like the same extent and the nature of the work really changed. Most people didn't like welding, There were famous incidents of Liberty Ships breaking in half and we saw in Lamont's a MacBrayne ferry that had been welded and it looked really terrible. So it was really only after the war that welding started to become popular. The conditions in the yards though were really terrible. In bad weather, when it rained, at the side of the boat you'd be up to your ankles in mud. Given that we started the boat, laying the keel blocks, and the shoaring, we tended to use old plates otherwise the shell squad wouldn't have got anywhere, the bogeys carrying the punched plates would sink up to their axles in mud. Management didn't want to do anything apart from making money. They certainly didn't want to lay out any money on the yards.

Joe Craig
Managing Director, Marathon Shipbuilding Co Ltd

I actually started my apprenticeship in Paisley at a company called Thomas Reid & Sons, now defunct, which made ship deck machinery. Then I went to Rolls Royce after doing National Service. I was trained as an engineer. I did two years at Rolls Royce and then got a job at John Brown's in the gas turbine division. I was offered a job by the then director in the works in the management. So I went out and got some qualifications. There was a course running at Glasgow Tech at the time on fabrication and I sat that and then went on to the Institute of Welding and a few other things, metallurgy, etc. When the North Sea Oil business started up, John Brown's diversified into this work at Rothesay Dock and I went there as Manufacturing Director. After a few years of fairly successful business, there was a slump in the industry and it began to look as if we'd be closing up. Coincidentally at the time I was offered a job of Managing Director of Marathon Shipbuilding which had taken over the John Brown yard as a consequence of the fall-out from Upper Clyde Shipbuilders.

Many of us were very conscious of the fact that John Brown's had taken huge losses on some contracts and that other yards which were to form UCS were also loss-making and that these losses would be carried over into the new firm. But at that time, industry had become a political battlefield. Although the unions had been created to protect themselves from exploitation, they had become exploiters themselves. They had also become very tribal, fighting amongst themselves, and demarcation was only one expression of that. There was no way that with the Japanese and others becoming both proficient and efficient in shipbuilding that we could compete with that sort of industrial turmoil going on.

Marathon was a completely different entity. The first thing they did was to restructure the yard to suit their products. They had customers in the States, in the Gulf of Mexico and it was two years or so before I got fully involved. The Labour Govern-ment had set up the British National Oil Corporation, a state-run company to exploit North Sea Oil. Marathon got work from them and then other clients and companies came in and we had a good run of work. Something, though, was happening in the parent company in the United States. Their directors were anxious to sell out to another company, a railway company, but they were very nervous about the trade union issue in Britain, seeing it as a situation of tremendous unrest, a tradi-tional American view. So I was heavily involved in that, trying to negotiate on the basis that things weren't as bad as they thought. I was also heavily involved in getting UiE to take over from Marathon.

Under UIE, we started to build modules and other top-side work for the North Sea, which was another change in the nature of the business. The rigs which we'd done before, jack-up rigs, were in between the building styles of shipbuilding and offshore, but once you went on to oilfield production problems it was a completely different style of contract with much higher technical standards and tighter forms of cost control. After I left, UIE really became a contract yard. It's a very cyclical business, with a base load of employment and workers coming and going as per the work. I feel very sad looking at the river now, the decline is, no doubt, a very complex issue but even in the sixties, the number of yards, the employment, and the issues of demarcation were problems. But it was always a battle, management and unions, unions amongst themselves, with every minor change being argued about and in some cases fought over. I don't know if everyone would agree with that but there were faults on both sides. If management and unions had both been brilliant I think we could have made a better fight of it, although it's impossible to say how we would have fared. Developing countries do seem to regard shipbuilding as important in their growth so that competition would still have been there.

Stuart Crawford
Electrician, Yarrow Shipbuilders Ltd

I started in Yarrow's about 1964 as an office boy, delivering messages and such like. I did that for a year and then became an apprentice electrician and worked on until 1969 when I left. I didn't have any family in shipbuilding as such but some in engineering but I wanted to be an electrician. Back then when you applied for a job you'd maybe get four or five offers but this was the only place that offered me a job as an electrician. I worked in various places outside the industry but I also did a stint at Scott's of Greenock and then came back to Yarrow's. I couldn't honestly say I was attracted back in, but one thing it did have in its favour was a continuity of work. The wages weren't too bad at the time, although they're pretty poor now. I lived locally so the travelling was easy. Having said that, you couldn't say that there was much about the industry that would attract, although I couldn't say there was much about other industries that I found attractive either. It was just a job.

Our trade hasn't really changed that much, it's one of the few trades in the industry where the type of work we've done has remained reasonably constant. Huge changes have occurred in the steelwork side, but in terms of outfitting, the type of work, the nature of the work and the way we do that work hasn't really changed that much. The big change is that we do a lot of the work before the ship is launched whereas in the past most of the work would have been done after the launch. The information we get is probably a bit better now than in the past but the fact is that the information should be a lot better and it's probably one of the failings in the industry. Getting proper information through to people on the shop floor still remains a problem. There's a sort of experiment, that's the only way you can describe it, attempting to graft on techniques from other manufacturing industries, systems engineers, process engineers and such like. The thinking behind this though, seems to be that building ships and making cornflake boxes, are the same sort of thing. You get one system into place and that fits with another system and so on but building ships isn't like that, never has been and never will be. You don't do runs of ships. For example, a huge order would be say three ships for us. But even then each individual ship will be different, they get modified constantly, so to try and graft on techniques and principles from mass production industry just seems nonsensical. But, those running the show seem to think that this is the way to go so let's hope they're right and that I'm wrong, because if I'm right then he's wrong and there will be a lot of trouble.

I don't feel secure in this job at all, indeed this is probably the most insecure I've felt in the last ten years. We've gone through some rough times indeed, we've been at rock bottom. During the time I've been convenor we've faced the threat of closure twice but I was always convinced that we would get orders. The orders were available, it was a matter of obtaining them, making the necessary changes to make us more productive.

It's a strange industry to work in, even people who only work in it briefly never seem to forget it. Mind you, the only people who have a burning to desire to work in shipbuilding are the sons of shipbuilders, owners that is. I'll maybe get a taxi to go to a meeting or something and the driver will say 'I remember you, you were the convenor in Yarrow's' and then they start telling you about what's going on. They are always interested in Yarrow's because it is in the paper or on the TV. The job itself is absolutely miserable and what makes it bearable is the people you work with.

Lynn Davidones
Ship's cleaner, Govan Shipbuilders Ltd

I started about sixteen years ago. It was very temporary, it was in between college and I was only there for about six to nine months. What happened was that my boyfriend at the times' mother and uncles worked in the yard which everybody called Fairfield's but it was of course Govan Shipbuilders by then. His mother knew that I could do with the money. So, having been at college and having worked in offices, there I was in this shipyard and it was just totally different. That's how I got started. I felt a bit scared when I first went in, just the size of the place, the noise and all these men welding round about you. It was an odd thing because I needed the work and she'd said to me a couple of times about this and I'd sort of shied away but eventually I took it and the money was really good. I didn't have to go for an interview or anything like that, it was a really casual thing, there was a guy who seemed to get all of these things organised and that was that.

I'm not sure how you would define the job. I suppose you could call it a cleaner or a labourer. We started off when I went onto the ship. The first job was stripping the cellophane off the panels and there were different kinds of panels, some wood, some formica, veneer and so on. We were mostly in cabins, although they didn't look like cabins at the time. It was amazing how quickly they took shape. Toilets went in, and again it was a case of stripping and cleaning and whatever was put in we had the job of getting it right and sometimes there would be guys welding beside us and we'd be scraping and cleaning right beside them.

We did get issued with boiler suits and big industrial boots and we did get face masks as well, I think because of the amount of asbestos which went into some ships but we never got hard hats. I remember they used to say watch out for certain types of hats, I can't remember now which was which red, blue or white. I think it was white for management. They were the ones you were always supposed to watch out for. Eventually this great thing came complete with beds in the cabins and we had to sort those out and I went out on the trial trip. I can't remember how far we went, but basically down the Clyde and back up again. After that we had to work down in Greenock and we were all taken down and back again on a coach and that lasted for about three weeks.

The work was basically the same but the ship was a great deal more advanced and by the time we finished down there the ship looked really lovely. The difference between the ship I'd first gone onto and the ship I'd left was quite incredible, you couldn't really believe what had transpired.

I only worked on the one ship but seeing that from what seemed to me a mess to the final product was just amazing. It was all women in the work that we did, there were about ten of us. There was an older chap who told us what to do, but it was definitely seen as 'women's work'. It was often a very early start and you'd be there to all hours so sometimes I'd just go home and go to sleep. When you say cleaning, it doesn't sound a lot but it was really hard physical labour. The compensation was that the pay was good, very good. Most of the men working round about were nice and friendly. I did pick up an admirer and I got a dozen red roses on three occasions and just before I left I got a letter with a telephone number. I got lots of chaff in the canteen but I never phoned that number.

Alex Dickie
Safety Officer, Fairfield Shipbuilding & Engineering Co Ltd

I started off in Fairfield before the war and did about three years there as a liner-off. When the war started, I joined the RAF and of course went all over the world. Then it was back to the yard and after a time, I got paid off and that's when I went to work at Thermotank, the ventilation and air conditioning company. I worked there for about three years. I didn't like it because it was noisy, so I got back into the yard again. It was quite a family thing, my young brother was an engineer, my uncle Alec was also an engineer and my uncle James also worked there.

After about seven years I heard that the safety officer was getting paid off as he was about 72. So I spoke to Mr Kimber, the yard manager, and he said to me 'we're booting the safety officer's arse out the door, would you like the job?' Anyway, I got the job, and I was sent here and there to get qualifications in safety work, and that started it off. I got on all right with Kimber and Lenighan, the Managing Director. But basically, once I got through my training, the job was more or less dealing with accidents.

I remember we had an explosion in Govan dry dock on the cruiser *Blake*. Quite a few were maimed. Once you investigate the accident you find out the cause. The men were taking their tea right down in the bottom of the ship and they went away after they'd finished not realising they'd left the acetelyne gas on. When they went down in the morning there was about ten of them in a place the size of a small room, they were smoking and having a cup of tea and somebody threw a cigarette away into a space where the gas had gathered. It wasn't only them that got burnt, the flames went through the trunking and into other spaces as well.

There was a ship manager. He was going down one of the ladders to get to the next deck through a hatch. He got a grasp of the hatch cover and brought it down on his head jamming him like a collar. Because he was badly injured, it made Kimber

and every one of them take safety seriously. It was a breakthrough.

This guy had gone down into the double bottom of a ship looking for faults in a tank. He had no lights or torch. Then another squad came along to test the tank and make sure it was watertight. They do this by flooding it up with water. They put the manhole on and screwed it all up. Then they turned the hose on, and it was only the water seeping underneath this guy's feet, that alerted him. When he eventually came out he was screaming blue murder. It should not have happened but the squad fitted the manhole because there were no temporary light fittings leading into the space so they surmised that there was nobody in there. He was lucky. With accidents you've got to write to the different departments and tell them that there is now a safety procedure for this. No matter what it is, if it's tank testing you must go down into the tank to make sure no one is in there.

It was a battle – you were fighting against people. The older guys that had been in for a long time and who wouldn't change. This was what happened to the old safety officer. It got him down.

I sat in on boardroom meetings where they're on about cost savings saying there's too much of this, too much of that, and so on but never once was told I couldn't get anything. I got all the safety equipment I needed, helmets, ear-muffs, shoes with steel toe caps and different things. It was one of those jobs where you're trying to push departments into being safety conscious. Up in the training centre I used to lecture them. I said to Kimber, I'm getting fed up, I'm not getting support. I'd like to get the managers and assistant managers and foremen up in the training centre, and that was a wee bit of a breakthrough.

I wouldn't check someone for doing something wrong, I would go to his foreman and tell him to do it, because otherwise you get into fights or arguments.

(Alex Dickie is the husband of Isabel Dickie p44/45)

Bob Dickie
Joiner, John Brown & Co Ltd

In August 1948 I began as an apprentice joiner in John Brown's. I had a brother who was a driller in the yard but he left in 1949. My father was a baker and he worked for a company which manufactured MacGregor's Fish Dressing. My mother insisted that there was no way that I was going into the bakehouse, so the obvious thing in Clydebank when you left school at 14 was to go into Singer's or John Brown's. I was fortunate enough to go into John Brown's.

When I started in the yard, the joiners' shop alone had something in the region of a hundred and ten to a hundred and twenty apprentices, which was fantastic by today's standards. I served my five years and when my apprenticeship was out I had to do my National Service. I did two years in the RAF and when I was demobbed I came back to the yard and stayed in there until 1996.

During that period I became shop steward for the joiners department, eventually became the convenor of the shop stewards and was convenor during the UCS work-in. I resigned in about 1976 from the shop stewards job and went back to the joinery. At that time the whole business had changed from shipbuilding to oilrig building. When UIE came into the yard in 1980, they wanted to subcontract the joinery work, so I was fortunate to get a job in the warehouse, being assistant stores manager and eventually became stores manager in 1987, and that was my job until I retired in 1996.

The joiners' shop in John Brown's made the furniture and bulkheads for all of the ships. When it came to the really big ships, the work in the public rooms tended to be contracted out but as far as furniture for cabins and passageways was concerned that was all done in the joiners' shop. We also did the bulkheads, a lot were Formica and we had our own veneer press for that. Most of the time I worked at the bench in the shop but after a while I went down to do what was called marking off, which was multiple jobs, supplying the material for joiners working on the benches. From time to time you'd be transferred from the shop out to the ship, mostly towards the end of the contract, in an effort to get it completed on time.

There was a sense of crisis however even before the UCS work-in. A lot of us felt that certain promises had been made about amounts of money being put in. There would be no redundancies, and you couldn't really believe that because shipbuilding just wasn't that sort of industry. It was peaks and troughs and we were all concerned about that.

A lot of good was done during the UCS period, industrial relations were good, wages and conditions were better, but there was always the feeling at the back of your mind that it wouldn't last. Some of us felt that bringing in people without shipbuilding backgrounds, Tony Hepper the Chairman and a chap called Duff, for example, were mistakes. It was only when Ken Douglas came from Austin and Pickersgill that we felt that we had someone who knew about shipbuilding. But there were always problems, ships taken at losses, that sort of thing and some of us felt that something was going to happen. At that time you had the situation with Rolls Royce, which was one of the blue chip industries, so if a disaster could strike there it could strike anywhere.

The one thing that stays with me is the atmosphere in the yard and the people in the place, even with all the problems you had between the different trades, demarcation and that, it was usually good and there were all sorts of characters.

(Bob Dickie is the husband of Isabel Dickie p42/43)

Isabel Dickie
Wages clerkess, John Brown & Co Ltd

I started in April 1945 as an office girl and I was the only office girl in the whole yard. The reason that I got the job was that my mother was friendly with a Mr and Mrs MacFarlane and he was the works manager. I was taken along one night to a big house on the Glasgow Road, it's still there actually, to be interviewed by Mr MacFarlane. I was fourteen years of age and absolutely quaking in my shoes. Anyway, he said to me when can you start? I think that I'd left school that Friday and by Monday I had started in the shipyard. I went in there on the Monday morning and I got taken up to this office and the general reaction was, 'what do we have to do with her?' to which the response was, 'Mr MacFarlane sent her in, she's an office girl'. So that was me started at fourteen years of age, working among thousands of men.

I stayed there for five years and left when I was nineteen, I got a bit bored with the yard and I went to Littlewoods football pools and was there for eight years. But that was the worst thing I ever did, it was an absolute slave shop with no unions. You would have a meeting with management once a month to air your grievances, but it was an absolute sweat shop and eventually I left.

I went back in to John Brown's when I was thirty-five, about 1966. I met one of the men I used to work beside, years before, and he asked me what I was doing and I said that I wasn't working. My daughter was about eight by then and he said he could get me a wee job on the Friday doing the wages. So I went back in one day a week and then they roped me in to the punch-room, two nights a week keying-in and that was me until I got paid off during the UCS work-in. I was involved with that for about a year and a half. We made up the wages, in fact we did everything for the work-in, including the balance sheets. Liz did

the typing and I did the wages, and then there was Margaret – I can't remember what Margaret did, she just got in the road half the time. Anyway, that's what I did for a year and a half, and then, when Marathon, the Americans, came in they wanted to interview for punching again. We had to go through a test and we did that with flying colours. I started with Marathon and worked there until I was made redundant in 1987. I was then phoned up and asked if I would come back. By this time they had a computer room and there was just Liz and I. I'd been unemployed for a year, so I didn't want to go back in full-time so I went in part-time, until I retired eight years ago.

When I first started in the yard, I used to have the job of making tea in the morning. I used to take the kettle every morning to the fire station and fill it up. Skiffington's office, he was the Shipyard Director, was up above the route I used to take. Miss Waugh said to me one morning, 'Isabel there's been a complaint about you'. I said, 'Oh, what have I done?' and I was all nervous about it, I still had ankle socks and a ribbon in my hair! And she said that Mr Skiffington had said that, 'There's a fair-haired girl goes down every morning at ten o'clock with a kettle to the fire station and I want to know why?' So we were told to stop doing that. Ultimately we clubbed together and bought an electric kettle and just made tea in the office but Skiffington didn't think anybody should be walking about the yard with a kettle in their hand. He was a hard taskmaster.

When I started you only got ten days off in the whole year and you worked on a Saturday morning. It was a very masculine environment but most of the men were cheery. I met my husband, Robert, in the yard. Although it was always an uncertain industry, there were jobs, good jobs, but you look at the river now and the overwhelming feeling is one of sadness.

Isabel Dickie
Dilutee Electrician, John Brown & Co Ltd

I started in the yard, John Brown & Co, around the time that my husband went overseas, so that would be around March 1942 when we were called up. I didn't go voluntarily, it was either the yards or the forces and I didn't want to go into the forces so I was put in the yards. I was a 'fancy' box maker in Govan at the time. You could have been sent anywhere, Aberdeen, Dundee, wherever, so I thought that I was quite lucky getting into John Brown's at Clydebank. I did six weeks training to become an electrician – that's dilution for you!

My family, and Alex my husband, both had backgrounds in shipbuilding. My father worked in Stephen's at Linthouse and then got a job in Thermotank where he used to go around all the yards doing work on ventilation and such like. I was eighteen when I started at Browns and despite the fact that the training was only six weeks I didn't do too badly. I learned Morse Code at Stow College where there were three shifts, morning, afternoon and night. You were really trained to do a very specific job which was what you'd end up doing in the yard. It was alright for a while but then the men got fly to it all and started to farm out the work to the women. I was in the yard for about four and a half years.

After I got married, I went back to the yard. We were married in May 1945 and I was in for a while out of necessity, we needed the money. The travelling was a killer though, I had to get down to Govan Cross and get the subway and then get the train down to Clydebank. I stayed with my parents when Alex was away, but mind you, there was no living together then, you didn't do that. My father travelled down to Brown's and Denny's but they were all bowler hat men – not like me.

The men were alright to us. But there did seem to be an attitude that we should do more work, but it was really heavy work pulling cables through. The cables were really thick and you had to pull then through the cabins. I didn't really bother with the men to begin with, I just did my job and got on with it. The squad that I worked in was all girls and they used to say that the electricians' squad were all snobs because we kept ourselves to ourselves. There were lots of women in the yard, cleaners, helpers, office staff, people in the canteen, electricians and rivet heaters. The cleaners were a right rough crowd mind, so we didn't associate with them. They'd try and get any man in the yard to take them out to save a bit of money.

I worked on a few destroyers but the ship I remember best was the aircraft carrier *Indefatigable*. As well as hauling cables we would wire up the Morse Code sets and the electrics in the gun turrets. The work could be really heavy, hauling cables in really awkward places but you couldn't really say the conditions were bad. We had our own toilets and our own canteen where you had your lunch. Given the circumstances you couldn't say it was too bad. War was war. Most of the time I was working inside so I missed the worst of the weather.

Sometimes it was quite difficult reading the plans, you worried about that, but you got there in the end. I loved the launches as you'd get to watch them and if it was late in the afternoon, you'd sometimes get away early. I used to work eight to five but I'd do a lot of overtime as we were saving up to get married, so I'd do Sundays as well. It was good money, there were women in all sorts of other jobs who wouldn't be getting anything near the money we were making. Sometimes you'd be up all night with the bombing and you'd be half asleep going to work. Clydebank was blitzed while my dad was working there. He met a woman walking up the street carrying a baby with no head and he sat down and cried something terrible that night.

John Dodds
Electrical draughtsman, Fairfield Shipbuilding & Engineering Co Ltd

As a youngster it was never my intention to work in the ship-building industry. However, leaving school at quite an early age on account of my parents dying, I managed to get a job in Rothesay in the electrical power station. It was quite a variety of work that they gave me to do, reviewing street lighting, controlling the fairy lights for the summer along the Rothesay front, and working with the electrical power generators on the switchboard. However the time came for my brothers and sisters to leave Rothesay and we came to Glasgow and settled in the Shawlands area. Through a friend I was recommended to Fairfield's shipyard in Govan, It was a Mr Skinner, head of the electrical department at that time who interviewed me. He took me in as a third year apprentice. Start on Monday morning at 8 o'clock. Report to the electrical office at the dockside, and a Mr Adam will meet with you there.

On Monday morning I made my way through the yard and eventually found the electrical office by the dockside. I was told that Mr Adam was on the ship, HMS *Woolwich*, and if I went aboard one of the workmen on the ship would direct me to where Mr Adam's office was. So I made my way on to the ship which was quite thrilling to be on a ship under construction. You had to be very careful walking along the decks, open spaces and cables were everywhere. I went down one or two gangways and saw this room marked electrical office. I knocked on the door and a voice shouted, come in, so I went in and said who I was. Aye, he said, what is it you're wanting? And I said, well, I've been told I have to get a job here as an electrician. Well, he said, if you just stand outside the door, I'll call you in a few minutes, I'm busy here with one or two men. So I stood outside, and after quite a long time, I shouted in the door, I'm not here for a long stand, I'm here to work. So Mr Adams called me in again, aye, he said, I can see that you're alright, I'm putting you along with one of the journeymen, and you'll go with him wherever he is on the ship.

So I was put along with a journeyman whose name I can't

recall. The type of work that I was engaged in was very interesting, fitting up fans on the decks of ships, wiring cabins, even up as far as the bridge, Not being a man who cursed, I got plenty of curses made at me when I was having to hold up heavy items of equipment. For example, on passenger liners overhead fans had to be fitted to the deck head. My job was to stand on scaffolding and hold that fan up while another man beside me bolted the fan on. I got plenty of curses when my hands started to shake but I just took it and never said anything back. That was part of the job and I accepted it and went along with it.

By this time I had put in a couple of years on the ships and I was transferred to the drawing office. I now had to produce on paper the work I had been doing on the ship. Quite often I was sent back down to the ship with a layout of where cable runs should be, and I had to follow these runs and mark up the cables, come back to the drawing office and put it on paper. So that was the sort of general run of my work.

Working at Fairfield's was quite an experience for me, having come from a quiet island to a busy city, amongst some men who were an element I hadn't been brought up with. At lunchtime, of course, some of the men went out to the local pub for a refreshment and had their lunch there, whereas I went over to the blacksmiths' shop where a number of us went and toasted our bread over the blacksmiths' fires.

During my drawing office days, quite a few of us made our way to Elder Park, and sat there or even played bowls in the summer time, and had competitions between the different departments, electrical office against the ship-drawing office or against the engine-drawing office.

I'm not a man who moves around, although I encouraged young lads I worked with to get out and enlarge their experience. I'm still in touch with one of them who is out in New Zealand. But I am not one for shifting around. I was 44 years in one yard. I don't think there are many who did as long as that, but I enjoyed it and I found it to be a great experience.

John Dollan
Plater, Yarrow Shipbuilders Ltd

I started in Yarrow's in the middle of winter 1966 and finished my time in 1971. I was there for another two years and left to do various bits and pieces of engineering work, offshore and such like, for the next ten years or so. I came back to Yarrow's around 1982 and I've been here ever since. When I came back, there hadn't been massive changes, dirt floors and working out in the open. Since then, of course, there's been the big covered berth, modern machinery, modern building conditions such as construction by prefabricated sections rather than building from keel up on the slipway. I'm not so much involved on the tools now, more on the trade union side but I'm a plater by trade so there's been a number of changes to what I do. At one time you stuck to the plating but now you do your own burning and grinding and you also do your own welding, not just tack welding and your own drilling. But at the end of the day tradesmen are tradesmen, you cannot be a jack of all trades because if you are, you're a master of none. In here, although the company has pushed for all sorts of changes, we've tried to restrain too many of them. There's been a lot of changes in the preparation shop as well, whereas you had maybe eight or nine markers, you have one machine doing the job, so it's an industry that has certainly moved on, it's no longer a boiler suit and cloth cap industry. For example, it's now a very high tech operation at least compared with what it used to be like. When I started, you'd lay the keel, do the ribs, put the shell plates on and the whole thing would be built piecemeal whereas now the whole thing is built in modules in the module hall. It changed the nature of my job in that it made it a bit easier. You don't have as much pulling and hauling as you used to have, whereas before you'd be pulling shell plates into position, you still have to butt them, but it's much more modern, you don't have chain blocks – it tends to be done on rollers. These things are done in reasonably large pieces and then moved down into the module hall. From the hall they are taken down by transporters and laid on the keel. When I started my time, it used to take us about four years to build a frigate. You built the hull, then you launched it and then you started the fitting out. Now the ship is about eighty five per cent finished when it's launched with most of the electrical work and such like done and it's finished in between eighteen months and two years. That's been a major change.

At one time you were in a position to bargain if you didn't like your job. You would just chuck it and go next door and get a job. Now it's just not like that. When I started on the river you had Connell's, Fairfield's, Stephen's, Barclay Curle's, John Brown's, Scott's down the river, so you could move around and sell your labour to the highest bidder or even move away into the oil industry as I did for a time, but even these jobs are no longer as lucrative as they used to be. The problem is the nature of the industry. At one time there used to be a massive training school in here. When I started my time there was maybe a hundred apprentices but now there would be maybe twenty five to thirty. There is a high rate of application for apprenticeships but what you tend to find is that once they come into the yard and they're serving their time, they see opportunities for staff jobs and they don't tend to stay on the shop floor very long. They tend to go and get a staff job, a collar and tie, a clipboard and a bit of paper rather than climbing about double bottoms which, to me, is quite sensible really. But at the end of the day we're going to have a severe skill shortage. If this place was to go to the wall where do we go? There are no other shipyards so we would be on the scrapheap.

Sir Robert Easton
Managing Director, Yarrow Shipbuilders Ltd

My grandfather was a master shipwright from away back in the days of Portsmouth Dockyard. He was a Scot from the Borders and from a large farming family with very little money and he had trekked south although he did come back to Glasgow and ended his days as a foreman shipwright on the river. I had an uncle who was a blacksmith but that was the only connection that my family had with shipbuilding.

I started as a fitter apprentice in 1939 in the old Fairfield yard and I went to the Royal Technical College, now Strathclyde University, and then worked as an apprentice draughtsman later qualifying as a draughtsman. It was not a common move. In those days there was no such thing as a scheme of training. Some companies were advanced in their thinking and did train apprentices, but you worked so long in the blading department, so long in the turbine department, so long in the boiler department – you were basically shunted about from department to department. You would get a bit of paper from somebody or other, always handwritten in an old school jotter showing progress. They did have an examination for the drawing office in your third year and if you passed you got in. So I went into the drawing office and was put into a section commensurate with the exam result. I'm afraid to say that I was fairly high up and I got put into the destroyer section. That sort of ship, destroyers and frigates, have been mine ever since.

I left Fairfield's and went to Yarrow's in 1951, joining the estimating department. I then became Commercial and Sales Manager and then Director of the same department. We went in and out of UCS and at the time we weren't doing too well because of the methods of working, the attitudes of the unions and so on. I was brought in to be Deputy Managing Director to a chap called Ernie Norton who was the new Managing Director. Between us we tackled putting Yarrow's back on its feet again. Until about 1971/2 we worked 24 hours a day, plus nights, so to speak, and by 1972, we had Yarrow's back in the black. In that period we had to borrow £4 million from the banks to keep the company stable and we repaid every penny of that, plus interest. When we came out of UCS and had turned the company around and were making money again, we had a policy, unlike a number of other companies, of spending the money, so we built new module halls, new outfitting shops, new flame-cutting machinery, new engineering equipment etc. We re-sited departments so that men didn't have to walk from here to there to get the job done. Whereas in the old days a foreman would go and collect all the bits and pieces to let the man do the job, we said this'll never work, so we planned that packages of work would come to you, me, whoever and you would do the work. You didn't have to go looking for it so there was a great saving in time. We calculated that we were saving over £500,000 a year in just walking time.

We started to build ships in bits and pieces and we sent young engineers to Italy, Japan, Germany, Spain, the States. When they came back we took the best of these ideas with a wee touch of Scottish *nous* thrown in. We structured a new production technique. We eventually got to the stage, we had two berths where we could do three ships at a time. One ship nearly finished, one half-done and one starting in the shops, so you had the nearest thing possible to a production line in a shipyard. We had a target of getting eighty-five per cent of the ship completed before it went into the water and although we never quite achieved that we did get into the high seventies. It was done in the dry, the men enjoyed it and the savings were tremendous. What cost one for a job in the shop would cost ten on the berth and twenty on the water so we tried to ensure that most of the work was done as near the far end of the production line as possible. We'd also covered two of the basins so that even when the ship was launched again it was in the dry.

Hugh Hagan
Carpenter, James Lamont & Co

When I left school in 1975, I started in James Lamont's yard in Port Glasgow as an apprentice carpenter. In my first year, in common with the rest of the apprentices on the Lower Clyde, I was in the Scott Lithgow training centre in Greenock. I then went to the yard and did another three years as an apprentice carpenter in what was called the 'new work'. The top end of the yard was where the new building work was done, the bottom end of the yard was for repair work and you didn't serve your apprenticeship there. We were fairly unique in that in the final year of the apprenticeship James Lamont's closed and we were moved by agreement with the unions to the big section of ship repairing of Lamont's which was at the dock breast in Greenock. So we finished our apprenticeship there and I was kept on for two years.

I was then made redundant and I worked in various jobs for a time. I then got a job in Scott Lithgow's as a plater/shipwright, which was a different kettle of fish altogether. I think I got the job because I had shipwright on my union card but the sort of work I'd done at Lamont's was almost solely with wood and this was totally different.

For a great deal of time I was on what was called shoar patrol, working under the boat shoaring, making sure there were sufficient shoars to support the boat. We were responsible for safety as well, making sure there were sufficient stanchions and adequate protection around the various holds and apertures on the deck of the ship. We were also responsible for the belting on the ship – saying this it sounds as if it was a thousand years ago – a wooden buffer which went completely around the ship, and we were responsible for making that, fitting it and securing

it. So coming from that to Scott Lithgow was a bit of a culture shock,

It was a new world to me, it was frightening, it was huge and it was big metal hammers and iron wedges and I wasn't used to that. Lamont's maybe employed about three hundred folk and your work would take you all over the yard whereas in Scott Lithgow there were thousands and you never moved out of the shed. You never really saw much of the rest of the yard.

There was certainly a feeling, amongst my generation at least, those of us who started in the 1970s, that things were being run down, certainly in the yards that I worked in. People were beginning to scratch around looking for other jobs, the older men, the people that were there when we started. It was at that time that places like Ardersier were taking off up north and the oil industry was booming with steel fabrication and the like and a lot of people were looking for jobs up there so you did get the feeling that the ball was burst.

There's a lot of images that stay with you. I remember the top shed at the Kingston yard where there was a big partition wall with a gateway into the bottom shed. Written right across the top of the gate in huge letters was the slogan 'Keep Kingston Protestant'.

I felt very sad when I walked out on my last day and still do. People may think that you're off your head but I really do miss a lot of what used to happen in the yards. It was really good crack and great camaraderie. It had its explosive side but there was a real community feeling which I think has now gone completely. I sometimes wonder if Scott Lithgow had flourished whether I would still be in the yard and I think the answer has to be yes.

Hugh Hagan
Welder, William Hamilton & Co

I started in 1948 in a yard called William Hamilton's and I was an apprentice welder. I was half way through my time when I got my draft papers for National Service, did two years in the air force and came back to welding. When I came back I went to the Kingston yard. There used to be three yards there, Duncan's, Hamilton's and Scotts at Kingston. At that time it was piece-work and invariably you found out, when you got your tally's on a Thursday, that your money wasn't right, so you had arguments, went to see the foreman, that sort of business. When this happened to you, you'd normally just lift your books and go elsewhere and you could do that then because there was plenty of work. So I worked in all five yards in Port Glasgow and I also worked in the Klondyke, Cartsdyke, which was the name given to the Greenock Dockyard. I also worked in Scott's which was further down the river and also up in Fairfield's at Govan, so I had a varied life in the shipyards.

Most of the yards had similar management styles, all rather Victorian. For instance when Ross Belch came into Hamilton's in 1949 or something like that, he wore a bowler hat and that was the type of management style they had. Although they suffered the unions, they just believed that you were there to work.

The piecework situation at the time was ridiculous because there were certain jobs you just couldn't make money at. You had the fall-back rate and come Thursday the saying was, 'my tally's down', and the foreman would say, 'well you didn't do this or you didn't do that so take it or leave it'. It continued like that up into the 1970s. When we were building the big super-tankers, we saw one day about eight or nine Koreans walking around on the deck of the ship and they all had notebooks taking notes about this and that. We eventually found out that they were paying Lithgows money to train these people to build these types of ships. That led in turn to Korea building these ships and us being told it was our fault because we were a lazy shower of so and so's who weren't doing our job. It just went from bad to worse.

Things improved a bit when British Shipbuilders came on the scene, but there was consistent change in management and there were faults on our side too, because we stuck to the trade union rule book. It was one man for one job when management were looking for integration of trades. I think if demarcation had been relaxed earlier things might have improved.

I've often said I'm not all that sorry that shipbuilding isn't there anymore because it was one terrible bloody job. The conditions and wages were rubbish and there's a lot of people yet in the town either dying or disabled because of that industry. The only thing is that nothing has come in its place.

I finished up here in Ferguson's in the 1970s, and retired in 1989. It wasn't my intention to finish but like everywhere else we were getting into bother with work. The Tory government at the time said they'd no objection to the yard staying open but not under British Shipbuilders, so if nobody bought it, it would close. At the time, I was shop stewards' convenor and we spent over a year trying to get the best deal we could. There were all sorts of people putting in bids, real fly-by-night stuff. So I finished up in 1989 when I was fifty-six and I haven't worked since. What you find then is that you're over the hill as far as work is concerned. People are very nice to you, say they're really sorry, fill in this form, etc, so when I turned sixty-five that was that.

(Hugh Hagan is the father of Hugh Hagan p52/53 and Paul Hagan p56/57)

Paul Hagan
Caulker/Burner, Ferguson Ltd

I had a whole family in shipbuilding. My grandad, my father, my brother and I had heard all the stories and the like and yet I still went into the industry! I started my time in 1984 in Ferguson's. I went to the training centre for four years. Well, the first year was the training centre and the rest of the time was a mix of in the yard and college as well as day release.

I served my time as a caulker burner, although they don't do as much on the caulking side these days. That was more a thing of the past and all you do now is a bit of chipping as it's called, taking off a bit of the weld that was loose. I mostly use the burning side these days. I worked in the sheds most of my time where you had computerised burning machines. You put a roll of computer tape into the machine and it cuts your shell plates, double bottom, bulkhead units, everything. It will cut to size, shape and anything that's to come out, like manholes, etc. After that I worked on the bar cutting machine which cuts bars to size and shape and cuts the brackets as well. There's a magic eye on the machine which runs round a template and if you put more or less any shape on that table, the machine will cut it and you get a really good cut. But they're updating even that now and the new machine has a plasma cutter on it and it works on a water bed and the cut is so clean you think the thing has just come out of a box. It looks perfect. It's really different from what I had when I started my time.

When I was at the training centre you did three months at a time doing the various trades, welding, plating, caulking/burning and then got picked for a trade. I must have been unlucky because I wasn't there on the day they got picked and I ended up in the caulking/burning department. I wouldn't say it's a bad department but a lot of people don't like it because it's so dirty and there's the heat from the burning, but I quite enjoy it. You feel as if you've done something at the end of the day. You can look back and say that was me, I did that.

The other side of the department is the water squad and I'm working there at the minute. They test all the tanks for leaks and do an air test and a water test. You pump the tank full of air and go round with a bucket of soapy water checking for leaks. The same with water. You fill the tank and because of the pressure of the water it can be a better test. That's what I'm doing at the moment and you can get soaked, like today, the bucket fell on top of me, covered me in soapy water.

There's a lot of good humour in the yard, loads of characters and that keeps you going half the time. The yards always seem to have had them. I worked up in Govan for a while and I was shop steward for the department and one of the meetings was to deal with a complaint about bootlaces being burnt out and a demand for leather laces! I never really liked Govan, it was too big, you felt lost and the sheds seemed black.

I think the industry still has a future, there's still plenty of work, the only problem is money. The problem is trying to compete but there's always going to be ships. Another problem is trying to get the men. We've only started four or five apprentices a year for the last five years and those who did work in the industry before are reluctant to go back.

Nan Hanlon
Secretary, Fairfield Shipbuilding & Engineering Co Ltd

When I started at Fairfield's in March 1966 I was working for Oliver Blanford who was the Managing Director. Even although I knew little enough about shipbuilding, you could tell that the rest of the Clyde shipbuilders didn't like what was going on. There was a resentment there, I think, because Oliver Blanford and Jim Houston, who had come in from Singer's, and who was the Production Manager, hadn't had anything to do with shipbuilding before. True, Mr Blanford came from Stephen's but he was on the engine side rather than shipbuilding. Mr Houston was not liked by many people because he used to say that it didn't matter whether you were making safety pins or building ships the management principles were the same and that rubbed many people up the wrong way.

Ian Stewart was in and out of Fairfield's all the time when I worked for Oliver Blanford, because he also ran Hall Thermotank. You did feel a sense of near permanent crisis, the Fairfield Experiment was supposed to be a three year experiment and Oliver Blanford was very very sorry that he didn't have the full three years to prove himself. He wasn't offered a place on the UCS Board and he went off down south. He was very, very bitter about that.

It was a shame that Fairfield's didn't really get the chance to show what they could do because there was such trouble with the unions, demarcation and all. When I first worked for Mr Hepper the offices of UCS were in Cadogan Street, in town. It was known as the Kremlin, but I think they became too expensive to run, and they had to watch the cash flow.

Sir Eric Yarrow withdrew from UCS before it went into liquidation. He hadn't been happy about going into UCS in the first place, I don't think, but he and Mr Hepper fell out about that and I don't think they ever spoke again. It was very dispiriting having gone through Fairfield's and UCS to see it all fail. I'd no job to go to when the liquidator, Robert Courtney Smith,

came in and asked me to work for him. But it was a strange thing working for the liquidator of a company which I'd been in for the whole of its existence.

I had met Sir Eric Yarrow when we had the Board Meetings at UCS and I think he knew that I would be unemployed once UCS was wound up. So I went to work for him until I retired in 1990. Actually I was made redundant. Sir Eric retired in 1986 so my world changed entirely and because I had been there for so long I was given a job working in public relations, but that only lasted for four years. Then we were taken over by the SEAMA Group and there were a lot of cutbacks, so at the age of fifty eight I was made redundant.

I couldn't believe it, me redundant. It was unbelievable. That was me finished but it was good while it lasted. I really enjoyed working at Yarrow's. It was a marvellous atmosphere and we had super offices that looked right out on the river. After a ship was launched they would bring it up to finish the fitting-out outside the office window and it gave me such pleasure to look out and see all these men working on the ship. All in all they were very nice people to work with, a lovely atmosphere and it had a real buzz about it.

When there were launches there was great excitement and I remember suggesting to Sir Eric once that he should get invitation cards printed to send out to guests but he said, no, no, they must have a personal letter. The trouble was, of course there were no word processors then. I had to sit and type every single letter, perhaps two to three hundred, and every letter was different. But that was the personal touch. The river now is so sad, there's no buzz about it now at all. It used to be that when you went down, 'doon the water' as they used to say, there was stacks of work going on, it was noisy, it was busy. It's a totally different world now. I feel sorry for the wee kids. It used to be exciting to go down the river but now it's so quiet.

John Innes
Engine estimator, Alexander Stephen & Co Ltd

I started off in April 1940 as a plan boy in the engine drawing office. What I wanted to do was to get into the shipbuilding side – I wanted to draw ships, that was my ambition. But the production manager said, no, you don't want to do that because there's a slump in shipbuilding. Engineering is more steady. Because of what he said, I started on the engine side. After I was sixteen I started in the engine shop as an apprentice fitter. The first department I went to was the blading department. At that time it was only turbines that were being built mainly, of course, for the Navy, There were a few merchant contracts as well, so the blading department was a very busy place. You went in there and you assisted the blader, made up the segments of blades which eventually were fitted on to the rotors and on to the casings. That was fine until about the end of September beginning of October 1940 when Stephen's, like many other yards, received orders for motor landing craft.

This was over and above the current production programme. This led to a shortage of fitters out in the yard to fit the diesel engines that came from America, and so many fitters and apprentices were taken out of the engine shops to work on the landing craft. That was good experience. But sometimes you had to ask for a move, because if you were working with a 'mate' who was quite happy to jog along and do the same thing on each ship that wasn't good experience for an apprentice. So you went to the chargehand or the foreman and they moved the boys around to get a wider view of the business.

So that lasted for a couple of years until March 1941 when there was an apprentice strike. The reason for the strike was that wage rates for 4th and 5th year apprentices were beginning to get out of proportion to what journeymen were getting. This applied particularly to 5th year boys who were really doing journeymen's work. They thought that they were getting a raw deal, in fact I think their rate at that time was 26/- a week.

But some of the men were probably earning £3 or £4 a week. So the district apprentice committee called a strike. I was in my second year, and thought this is terrible, a strike, but you just had to follow the band. But the strike coincided with the Clydebank Blitz which happened on Wednesday and Thursday night. On the Friday we went down to pick up our lying time and when we got down to the yard you couldn't get along the Govan Road because a landmine had demolished a tenement building right across from the engine shop.

The strike was very quickly settled. It was a case of just upping the wages a bit, up from 13/6 to 19/6. It was a big jump for me. Back in the yard the first job we got was to clear up the mess in the engine shop because the glazed roof had come down on to the machines. The place was in a terrible state. We spent about a week with brushes, getting the place tidied up.

After the war I worked in the drawing office right through to 1962. I would say it looked as if shipbuilding was going to last for ever. It was just one order after another, no problem. When I later went into the estimating department, there were loads of enquiries. We would select the enquiry we wanted to pursue. If it was for Swedish America, then we didn't want it. If it's for British Rail, we'd have a go and so on.

Stephen's was a very good company to work for in that sense, and there was a good camaraderie between everybody, even from the top of the house. Although Sir Murray and John Stephen were slightly aloof, they were good employers,

I always remember the day we were in a meeting with Jim Stephen. He was telling us about discussions on the proposed merger with Connell's and Yarrow's. The next thing this guy came rushing in and whispered something in Sandy's ear. Then Sandy stood up and said, 'sorry, we'll need to abort the meeting, one of the Russian dredgers is sinking'. Somebody had opened a valve which operated the suction pump and allowed water into the ship. That was the kind of thing that happened, that didn't need to happen.

Margaret Jeffray
Secretary, Scott & Sons Ltd

I started in 1970 at Scott & Sons of Bowling which became part of British Shipbuilders when the industry was nationalised. I left in 1980. My father worked with William Denny's at Dumbarton all his life. He was a marine engineer, and when Denny's closed down he went to John Brown's at Clydebank and worked on the *QE2*. He was there until he retired.

Initially I worked at the University but I wanted a job nearer Bowling and I happened to see one advertised so I applied for it and got the job. I wasn't put off by the fact that it was a shipyard. I was secretary to the Managing Director, but as well as working for him I also worked for the Company Secretary and the Yard Manager, as I was really the only secretary there. I was in charge of the general office but there was only one other typist there so the work was quite concentrated. At the time we were building fishery protection vessels for Mexico and we used to do repair work for the paddle steamer *Maid of the Loch* on Loch Lomond and the pleasure boat on Loch Katrine, *Sir Walter Scott*. That would involve repair and refit squads going up to the lochs and doing the work there.

The yard was small really so it specialised in building or repairing small vessels. Working for three different people made the job very varied. For the managing director and the yard manager the subject matter was very different and for the company secretary it tended to be mostly figure work. I didn't do the wages though, that was all handled by a manager.

Although it was a very male-dominated environment I really enjoyed my work and I liked the yard. I do remember though that there were quite a lot of Mexicans over when we had the fishery protection boats. A lot of them couldn't speak much English and they used to go to the Esso canteen, which is just along the road. We didn't have a canteen in the yard and the Mexican's would go to lunch with some of the men. They were friendly, the Mexicans, and I used to get to present the flowers to the wife of the boat's commander as they always did the launchings.

There was a nice family feel to the yard. I don't know much about the Scott family or whether they still had any connection with the yard when I was there, but the man who was the Managing Director had started off as an office boy and there were very few airs and graces about the place. I wouldn't have left had it not been closed. It was a really friendly place to work and I don't remember any trouble or any strikes.

I used to do things like typing up contracts and specifications, things like that, and of course, there were no computers then. It was a bit intimidating at first, you knew you couldn't make a mistake, but once you got used to it, it was pretty straightforward. On the office side there were only about seven people like myself and four managers. The yard didn't employ many people, some did come down from Glasgow but most people were from Bowling or Old Kilpatrick.

When the yard closed there were opportunities to go to Govan or Greenock but if you didn't have transport Greenock was an awful place to get to and a lot of people just didn't want to travel. I went to the union to work, the AUEW, after Scott's closed. I got the job twice actually, the first time I didn't take it and it appeared in the papers a few years after and I applied and got it.

Tom Jenkins
Shipyard Manager, Ailsa Troon Shipbuilders Ltd

I left school in 1960 and started with Fairlie Yacht Slip as an apprentice yacht builder. I worked there for four years and during that time it was mainly wooden yachts you were building but we built barges and landing craft for the Ministry of Defence. We built eight-metre yachts right down to the smallest class of yachts which at that time was the Loch Long.

It was good work, excellent work, and from there I went into the loft for a period of time during which I was going three nights a week to night school. The night school teacher asked me if I was interested in a job at Ardrossan Dockyard. At that time they were doing ship repair so I moved from Fairlie to Ardrossan, which was my home town, and effectively, I got taken into the drawing office and I was in there carrying out all sorts of wee draughting jobs. I was studying naval architecture at night school, but I immediately found that what I was studying at night I could apply during the day.

I spent four years with Ardrossan Dockyard and left there in 1968 as a design draughtsman and I started with Troon in October 1968, I went straight into the design office and they were building ships there, not repairing them. So I've actually been with this company in excess of thirty years. I started in management in my early thirties, as a planning manager, believe it or not, but I felt that I'd done my whack in the drawing office and needed more experience. We went from two building berths outside to a single berth under cover which meant that a yard of our size had to become a bit more disciplined in the approach to the overall building technique.

When I came here in 1968 there were about four hundred and fifty people working and in the early seventies we picked up work in a serious way. We went from the standard vessel being something like sixty to sixty five metres going up to ninety, ninety five metres and through to about 1976 the workforce went up to over seven hundred. Then it took a nose dive and

roundabout 1978 we got nationalised and, let's face it, nationalisation saved us from closure, there was no question about that. Life was bearable and there were an awful lot of good things that came out of nationalisation. Demarcation was dramatically reduced, productivity was improved and there was a lot of investment. But international conditions were really harsh and the government seemed to have it in for British Shipbuilders. What effectively happened was that this yard was scheduled for closure by the mid 1980s. We had a very strong local campaign to save the place and I happened to be the management representative on the 'Fight to Save Ailsa' Committee. There was five of us and I was pleased to be approached to help. I'd been here for years and I didn't feel as if I wanted to walk away from the place.

We went down to Westminster and conducted a wee campaign. We got closed effectively for something like ten days and by the end of 1986 we had managed to persuade British Shipbuilders to sell us off. We stumbled across a guy who was interested in taking the place on and essentially we worked it from there and by February 1987 we built up from ten people. It's been quite an enlightening experience. The workforce is now up to just over two hundred people, and all in all, supposing I left tomorrow, I'm still pleased that I was part of it all. What we're about is trying to maintain skill levels. The big problem for every yard and every heavy industry that's remaining in this country is that there's a skills gap now.

About eighteen months ago we started about seventeen apprentices, and I've got to say we've got something like fifteen left. But the average age in here is around the fifty mark and we've got to try and keep eating away at that and get it down. *(In the late summer of 2000, management gave notice that the shipyard was unable to trade profitably. The yard gates closed for the last time in December 2000.)*

George Kerr
Electrician, Scott's Shipbuilding & Engineering Co Ltd

I served my time in the contracting industry in a small electrical firm and I was attracted by the shipbuilding industry which was higher paid at the time. This would be the mid 1950s, and the first yard I joined was Scott's in Greenock. I was working on a Fleet Replenishment ship for the Navy and submarines for New Zealand. After a short period of time, in 1966, I got a job in Alexander Stephen's in Linthouse, which was just up the road from me.

The year before that, there was a national inquiry into shipbuilding in Britain and Geddes, the man who chaired the committee, suggested that there should be the grouping of shipbuilding on an esturial basis. On the upper river you had Upper Clyde Shipbuilders and down on the lower reaches you had Scott Lithgow. As part of that deal, Stephen's closed and I was transferred to Yarrow's. So I've seen many crisis points and changes in the industry. We've seen the decline of shipbuilding in Britain, from world leader, having a large percentage of world shipbuilding, to an infinitesimal number of ships being built by us.

I believe that if the industry shrinks any more it may not be able to sustain itself. The argument varies around a manufacturing base that now accounts for around fifteen to twenty per cent of the economy whereas the rest is financial, leisure and services. There must be a point where that base of manufacturing, the wealth creation sector, drops to such a point that it cannot sustain the economy. Nobody has ever tackled that issue. I've never seen any statistics, read anything that would tell me at what point that becomes a crisis and the whole economy implodes and collapses.

If you look at the decline in the basic industries in Britain – coal, steel, engineering, shipbuilding – all going to the wall, we seem to have let them go whereas everybody else appears to defend them. There needs to be recognition that we need a shipbuilding industry and measures to get ships back on to the British register, with encouragement for British flagged ships to be built in British yards.

I'm getting to an age now where I've spent nearly a lifetime in shipbuilding. Hindsight is always a perfect science, of course, but I do think that demarcation was a problem. There were always arguments over it. We scored, I would imagine, a number of own goals. Whilst our international competitors were working away, we were squabbling amongst ourselves.

So demarcation was a factor and not the major factor, not the key factor, in my opinion. Over the thirty two years that I've been in the industry there has been the lack of commitment by governments of all shades in terms of putting in resources. Look at Korea, built with Western capital and Western technology, some of our best shipbuilding technology went over there and people went with it. Japan totally rebuilt its industry after the War while we were left to get on with it with clapped out equipment. So we had to work twice as hard just to stand still. Subsidies were given to the Korean industry and I remember once the Govan yard trying to compete for an order which they couldn't even compete on the price of steel because of the subsidies.

The biggest change I've seen has to be modular building. The change from putting a keel down on an open slipway to building in large components and sections all under cover. When we've gone abroad on delegations and we're told that we are losing orders because of A, B or C, foreign workers didn't work any harder etc, they don't work any differently. So how do they get all the orders and we don't? It may be illegal in EU terms but it does seem to me that certain countries are prepared to do whatever is necessary to support their basic industries.

Charlie McIntyre
Rigger, John Brown & Co Ltd

I started in John Brown's in October 1943 to serve my time as an apprentice ship rigger. That was me from then right up until 1985. John Brown shipyard, the UCS, then Marathon.

Riggers worked with the wire and rope in the yard and on the ships. We also did all the maintenance work for the cranes. In fact, to be honest, as an ordinary lad working there, getting married and having five kids, it was a good job although my wife never saw much of me. If I wasn't working on a boat, I'd be doing maintenance work on the cranes Saturday and Sundays. It was a good paying job in that sense, although you had to put in a lot of work. No fly-by-night payments, just straightforward hours worked. I know it sounds funny but I loved it. A lot of people look at me as if I'm tuppence off the shilling, but I really loved getting up and going into work every morning because you could never say what you were going in to do. A welder would go in, and he'd maybe weld bulkheads, from morning to night, five, six or seven days a week, but we were never like that. We were down at the west yard one day, away at the east yard the next and maybe at the dock the day after that.

There were eight sons and three daughters in my family. I'm the seventh son. One died at birth. My oldest brother James was a plater, the next one, Bobby, a machineman, worked in Meechan's then he worked in Singer's. Andy was a shipwright in Barclay Curle's shipyard. He finished up the spar maker, which was a pretty skilled job prior to the war. He used a lot of really old fashioned tools like draw-knives and things like that. John was a blacksmith and Billy was a joiner. Tommy was the youngest. He did his National Service then came into John Brown's.

I remember when my wife Lily and I were just married and living down in the John Brown buildings near the Library in Clydebank and Tommy coming in with a wee parcel under his arm. He says that's me off to Australia, I've joined the Australian Army. I couldn't believe it. He'd been for medicals and all the rest of it. I didn't see him again for forty years.

I came out of school at 14, and the day I was leaving school, the headmaster gave me a letter. Just take that home to your father. In these days you didn't open it. So I took it home and gave him it. My mother had died when I was about nine, so he opened it and said, he wants you to go down to Dumbarton High School, St Patrick's in Dumbarton. He says, do you want to go? Being young, you say . . . oh no, I don't want to go. Andy's got me a job in Barclay's as a machine boy in the joiners' shop. So he says, well, it's up to you, just as long as you don't rue the day. But I went into Barclay's and I was there for about a year or something, then they brought girls in to work with machines. This would be 1941. By that time I would be maybe coming up for 15 and I was actually working a mortis machine. No such thing as a guard round it or anything.

Then they made me an apprentice joiner. You're supposed to be 16, but because of the war and that, I was made up. When I got my first week's wages as an apprentice, I was still getting the boy's wage. I think it was about 10/11p. So I went to see the foreman, a man called Morgan, a stockily-built man, with a round scar on his face. He said, you don't get the apprentice's wages until you're 16 so I said, keep your job. I walked out and started in a wee plumbers' shop and I was there for maybe a couple of years. By that time I was in the sea cadets when they first started in Clydebank. And I went down the Labour Exchange to see if I could get a job. My father said to me don't take a job in Singer's. They'll offer you Singer's, don't take a job there. It's a dead end place.

The officer in the sea cadets was Davy Martin, and he was the chargehand rigger in the yard at that time, so I went in and I remember it as though it were only yesterday, opening the door, The Rigger's Loft was up above an engineering shop. I was 17 at the time and I just felt at home right away. I always felt that way and I never looked back. When I started there were thirty two people in the loft, including the foreman, two chargehands, a storeman, a labourer, five apprentices, the rest being riggers.

Tom McKendrick
Loftsman, John Brown & Co Ltd

I was six years in the shipbuilding industry which spanned from being a plan boy to being a loftsman. A loftsman is a kind of draughtsman who draws everything out fullscale, and transfers it to wooden templates. I started when I was fifteen years of age. It's the classic thing: 'Dad, I want to be an artist.' 'Oh, so you think so? You get a trade behind you, son.' Looking back there was comfort in that, because the reality of the situation was that ships were big iron things, they're not going to disappear overnight, they weigh 76,000 tons. They had that feeling of permanence.

I always remember going down to Brown's for my interview and thinking, this is going to be terrible. A guy sat down and said, 'right, this is a test.' I sat writing it all out, and he lifted it up and looked at the bottom of the form and read, Braidfield High School. 'OK lad, start on Monday.' So off I went into this big place, it was like a pigeon loft. Hundreds of dookets full of plans, and the guy says, 'Right , you're in charge of this, you're a plan boy.' And I said, what do I do? 'You check the name of the man who takes the plan out and tick his name off when he brings it back, and put the plan back in the right box.' And I said how do I find the plans? 'Aw Christ, see that up there, that's the front of the boat, that bit down there's the bottom of the boat, that's the top, you'll soon find your way about.' He disappears and two minutes later a guy taps the door, 'Oh right, wee man, new start eh? Can you get me the plan for the bulk-head, on the chain deck, stringer 23, run number 42?' Thrown in at the deep end.

I had desert boots on which were very fashionable at the time, but not too hot in a shipyard. Someone says, you better get yourself a pair of boots, son, or your toes will not last any longer than a fortnight. I went to the security man. I need boots, and in these days you paid it at, I think, one and three-pence a week. As I'm going out the door the guy says to me, 'by the way son, see before you put them on, give them a right good doing with a hammer,' and I thought, I'm not ruining my new

boots, that's sick. I sat down and thought I'll put them on. One day's work running all over the yard with plans and when I got home that night, my boots were full of blood and my feet were destroyed. You learn the lesson very quickly. When somebody said something to you and you said I'm not doing that, they never turned round and explained it to you, they just went, fair enough. And you always paid a horrible price.

I got to know the yard back to front, running around with plans all the time. You could see how the managerial system worked: 'Aye you will do it. No I'm no doing it. You'll fuckin' do it. If you don't do it you're out in the morning.' They would always come into the plan office so they could shut the door and have a fight in private. And me sitting in my wee seat at one end, hoping the phone will go so I can go away with a plan.

Then circumstances overtake you. I wanted to be an artist so I was doodling on the back of the book. 'Son, you're no bad at drawing. Archy, come here to see this, I think we'll put him into the loft.' So I became a loftsman. It was ideal, but life is a learning curve. The very day, for instance, my apprenticeship was up, this guy, Hugh Montgomery, came up to me with a plan and says, 'right, that's you, you're time's out, there's your tool box, there's your job,' and he threw these drawings down in front of me. Ship number 731, mark the hull off for these intakes and I thought, Oho, and opened the drawing up. It was intakes on the side of the boat about 6 foot square for taking water from the engine room. I thought to myself, Aw naw, I'm standing right beside this boat and there's a burner, a plater, a guy with the big crane and a welder waiting for me to tell them where to cut this huge vent on the side of this boat. But you just had to go for it. The funny thing was that it was just assumed that you had learned your trade, there wasn't any check-up.

My dad's views about getting a trade were well founded, shipbuilding had been there for a hundred years. But in fact, after spending six years doing an apprenticeship and getting fully qualified, the whole thing collapsed two years later.

Colin McKenzie
Welder, Wm Simon & Co Ltd

I served my apprenticeship at Simon's at Renfrew and I started around 1949. I worked in the Blythswood and then moved to Fairfield's in 1956. I remember it well because it was the time of the Hungarian uprising and there were meetings outside the shipyard gates. Some men weren't too popular I can tell you. There was one day when a guy from the Communist Party nearly got lynched for supporting the Soviets.

I worked my time as a welder which seemed very much the coming trade at the time. I really liked working in Simon's and I would've stayed there all my time if I could have. I liked the type of work and I liked the people in the yard. You could say that I become a sort of Renfrew person whatever that might mean. I was six years in Simon's then went over to the Blythswood yard at Scotstoun, and then back over the river again to Fairfield's. After that it was all the way back over and down to Denny's at Dumbarton.

The main differences in the yards tended to be the types of ships that they built. Blythswood specialised in tankers, Denny's in ferries, Simon's in dredgers, while Fairfield was a more mixed product yard.

Although I really liked Simon's, it was probably the worst to work in. Really small, awkward confined spaces because of the nature of the ships they built. If you were to put a dog into some of the spaces that men were asked to weld in, you'd have the cruelty down on you. The extraction of fumes was really in its infancy then and we fought a long struggle to get fans introduced.

I applied for a job in Yarrow's and they put the bar up on me because of my trade union activity and it took me months to get in. They were supposed to be desperate for men and it ended up that Dan McGarvey, who was the leader of our union, met with Sir Eric because the Clyde district had, in turn, put a ban on any labour starting at Yarrow's until I could get a start.

I'd been a shop steward and had caused some hassle. We'd fought for work-sharing when Simon's first started to pay people off. There was a lot of argy-bargy about it. Men were going to be paid off while there was overtime being worked, so none of it made sense to me. Eventually we threatened a full scale overtime ban if anyone was sacked. So I don't suppose it made me too popular with the bosses.

Eventually, Simon's merged with Lobnitz although I was away by this time. I heard that they were then accepting what was termed 'run down money' which seemed daft as it was acceptance of the fact that the yard was being run down to closure. Eventually though I got the start in Yarrow's.

I never really felt that the industry was in any great shape in the whole of the post-war period. It seemed to me that it was sustained indirectly by international factors, the Korean War boom, the closures of the Suez Canal in 1956 and 1967. They all seemed to be semi-artificial stimulants which were masking the problems in the industry. I can well remember a manager in the Blythswood saying to us that it was going to get an awful lot harder to get orders. There would be a lot more competition and that it just wasn't going to be like the past.

Mind you, when I think about Yarrow's, when I first started there compared to other places that I'd worked in, the place seemed like a holiday camp. You did less work than any other place on the river. Did more walking about than working. That only really changed when GEC took it over. Bob Easton was the guy who transformed it, because he'd watched all this nonsense going on.

Roddy McKenzie
Welder, John Brown & Co Ltd

I had no family in the industry. In fact, my father was a butcher and he went into the trade after coming back from the First World War. I wasn't really attracted to shipbuilding but I wanted to serve my time in some trade. I went to plating, sheet iron work and engineering but when I saw the money that the journeymen welders were getting compared to other trades I said, that's for me.

I started at Meechan's in Scotstoun in 1944 and served my apprenticeship there. It was engineering and building lifeboats and I worked in there as an electric welder. I worked there until the War ended and then I moved into the shipyards. I went into Connell's first and then on to Stephen's and then to Harland and Wolff. After that I went abroad.

When I came back I went to John Brown's which I thought was the best yard of the lot as far as foremen, managers and workmanship went. The foremen were reasonably amicable and they had the best senior management on the Clyde personified by John Rannie. He was a marvellous managing director, knew everybody by name and knew what everyone was doing. Other managers in other yards would never look at you or talk to you.

The workmanship was a bit better than most inspection wise. Admittedly the *QE2* and the *Britannia* were a bit exceptional but by the time we got onto oil rig building, big Rannie and lots of the other managers had gone and there were lots of new managers, some of whom were OK. But others were really tragic as regards dealing with the men. Then they threatened to close the place and we had the work-in and that stopped the yard from closing. They went into oilrigs then and they're still

producing them yet.

I liked John Brown's out of all of the places I worked whether it was down south or abroad. It's funny, because Brown's was not a family yard in the sense of ownership but it did have a family feel. Maybe because lots of 'Bankies' worked in the place and everyone knew everyone else.

In terms of moving from other yards, it was normally the case of getting out before a launch to try and get a start somewhere else, rather than be unemployed for a week or so.

I did enjoy the travelling when I worked abroad. Mostly I did supervisory work in Iraq, Iran and Kuwait and went to Australia, just outside of Perth, but I didn't like Australia much! I preferred Scotland. I've been lucky never being unemployed and always able to get work.

It was gigantic then, the Clyde, all the shipyards right down to Greenock. They talk about having trouble with the unions and Red Clydeside but I never saw any of that. There is a lot of mythology about the UCS work-in and I should know because I was treasurer for the strike fund. We got donations from all over the world and it was the hardest thing I ever did, but every penny was accounted for.

The work-in was a necessity, you knew there was a sense of crisis in the industry. There was a sense that you were the last of a dying breed and if the yards had not been fought for, the Clyde would have been a total washout. I think the work-in was successful, yards are still building, Govan is still open, and if you think of the years since the work-in, that's employment that would have been lost otherwise.

Andrew McLauchlin
Outfit Manager, John Brown & Co Ltd

I started away back in 1937 and worked in the drawing office in John Brown's at Clydebank. I then went onto the production side of the business which is the actual process of building the ships. I went on to become Outfit Manager and then became Construction Manager. I retired in 1983. So really, my whole career was based on naval architecture.

My brother James was in shipbuilding and my other brother Willie was in the marine engineering side of the business. We lived in a shipbuilding town although my father was with the fire service and none of the family had been involved in any way with heavy industry. I did studies at the Royal Technical College in Glasgow and a course at the University and eventually ended up lecturing in naval architecture and marine engineering. Although I was not an engineer, I had sufficient knowledge of the subject which I could impart. My apprenticeship lasted five years and I was fortunate in that I was never paid off. Thankfully I worked all the days from when I started until I retired.

I also had some experience of foreign shipyards with ships that we had built which needed to be surveyed, particularly in Germany and Sweden. I was most impressed by almost all the Continental shipyards I visited. They weren't paragons of virtue and no doubt they had their lazy men just like us, but in comparison to the British, they were more inclined to put their shoulder to the wheel. The sort of thing I would look for would be what time they would appear for work in the morning. They were incredibly punctual.

I don't think that technology was the key difference, it was more of an attitude to work and there was no demarcation – they could turn their hand to anything. In Germany, I once saw journeymen finishing a job and then sweeping the deck behind him. That would never happen here, and it was this accumulation of little things that made a difference.

When Upper Clyde Shipbuilders began, there was some progress on relaxing demarcation but there was always something which would crop up that would mean that progress could only go so far and it was never eradicated. The whole problem of demarcation was that it was all about self-preservation. Certain people have said, 'we'll hold on to this and we'll hold on to that,' instead of taking the opportunities to spread the jobs and let everybody become involved. It was only when the oil-related work started to come into the yards that attitudes began to change particularly when the Americans took over to build oil rigs, or what they called 'the Big Cans'. There were different types of jobs and techniques and you had to be more adaptable, the workers had to function as a team.

It was amazing when we went out on the ships on sea trials. Everybody mucked in. You never heard, oh, I'm a joiner, or I'm a plumber. It was all done in a completely different atmosphere. But back in the yard it reverted to the same old thinking.

Here in the British Isles now there are no really big ships building although there are plenty on the Continent. When I look at the river now it's very sad. Even the big crane at Scott Lithgow has gone.

John McLean
Plater, Barclay Curle & Co Ltd

I started in shipbuilding in 1924. I was fourteen and I'd just left the school. The first job I did was working along with the plumbers. It was my brother that took me along. He was a plumber and I started in Barclay Curle's West yard at Scotstoun.

There were two other brothers who were platers, another who was a blacksmith and yet another who was a foreman shipwright at Stephen's.

I always remember the first ship that I worked on was a P&O boat, the *Cathay*. She was a liner and we also built her sister ship the *Comonin* at the Clydeholm yard. They were both launched on the same day on the same tide. There must have been thousands down to watch the launches.

I worked at Barclay's for a few years and then I decided that I wanted to be a plater so I left there and went to Barclay's other yard, Clydeholm at Whiteinch. I was going to start my apprenticeship there and somebody said to me, 'Look John, I don't advise you to start an apprenticeship there.' They specialised in oil tankers and there was a view, which seems funny now, that there was no future in that sort of vessel.

But I did go in to Clydeholm and served my time and after that I worked all along the river in many of the yards, working on all types and classes of ships, oil tankers, dredgers, liners, naval vessels, everything. Shipbuilding was our livelihood and it was a great industry to be in, you'd see the ship in the water after she was launched and then in the dock and to me there was great pride in seeing that finished article go down the river.

I went away to sea during the depression in the 1930s. Work was really hard to get and I had a relative who worked with the Donaldson Line out of the Clyde and he got me a start there. I was an ordinary seaman and then an able seaman, so I had two trades, plater and able seaman.

I came back in 1937 and I was working as a sheet-iron-worker out at Hillington Estate. It was still shipbuilding work though because it was sub-contracting work doing ventilation for ships. The first place that I got a job as a journeyman was in Harland and Wolff's in Govan and it was a good company to work for. I was doing brackets and angle irons – you would have squads doing shells, cassions, frames, bulkheads and others doing water tanks or whatever.

Sometimes in the morning you would go in and if the weather was good the sun would be shining through all the rivet holes in the plates casting all sorts of patterns on the ground. When the weather was bad though, you'd have all the rivet fires glowing brightly, rivets being flung in all directions, the men hammering and the noise was deafening. It was like a scene from Dante's Inferno.

One of the things that I can't understand is why we had to import a bunch of foreigners intent on closing bits of British industry down. You had Ian McGregor in steel and coal – they should have flung him down the first pit he went to. Then you had Graham Day who was an axeman at British Leyland and did a similar job in shipbuilding when he was chairman of British Shipbuilders. So we've hardly any steel, Ravenscraig has been demolished, one working pit, no motor industry and hardly any shipbuilding.

I finished up in 1976 working at Govan, the old Fairfield yard, and I worked there several times during my life. It was alright for the squads but a more difficult place if you were a jobbing plater. I was really sorry when I retired as I'd no idea what to do with myself. I was about 66 and I had intended to go until I was 70 but I had chest trouble through asbestos.

There was a lot of friendliness in the shipyards, a lot of good people in the yards, a lot of clever people.

Duncan McNeil MSP
Caulker, Scott Lithgow Ltd

I started in the Greenock Dockyard Company when I was 15. I came out of school like most people did in the area at the time and got a start. That would be about 1965. I started as a caulker's boy. That was the year before my apprenticeship started. There were loads of boys – welders' boys, plumbers' boys, whatever. Essentially you functioned as a sort of message boy running back and forward for a variety of things. You couldn't imagine now the terms and conditions. There were guys of 70 or 80 years of age in the place.

So that was my start. I was then in what was called the Klondyke. The basic rates were very similar and people chased overtime and went from one yard to another in an attempt to boost their earnings. The Cartsdyke yard was called the Klondyke because there was always good money to be made working overtime there. It also had a ship-repairing outfit attached to it so there was always a good bit of work there.

My starting as a caulker/burner coincided with an initiative in the industry known as the Shipbuilding Industry Training Board. Here you did a full year at college, not day release. We were taken completely out of the yard and I think that most people resented that at the time.

People tend to forget that the definition of caulking is 'to make watertight', so although the trade has changed hugely over the years there is still a very important role for caulking. Particularly so in tank testing where you have water and air tests done by the water squad and they would be responsible in ship repair for say portholes, doors, etc. I was at one time a 'soapy water boy'.

Nobody really thought that the industry could go into the catastrophic decline that it did, although the signs were probably there. We had people from Japan and Korea working with us, staying with us, as part of a learning process within the shipyard. They were obviously modifying what they saw to take back home. But in Greenock and Port Glasgow, with thousands and thousands of people employed in the industry, the idea that it would all totally disappear wasn't really in anyone's thinking.

Even when things became difficult on the Upper Clyde, the reaction to it was that the political clout that they carried was part of a process which could threaten governments. There were lots of dangers in this for politicians who would simply suggest shutting shipyards. But there was a political argument that we shouldn't have been involved in the battle for UCS. Their loss would be our gain on the Lower Reaches. There was a perception that we were making money and that this was an albatross up the river that was costing money and that we could have used that money better. So there wasn't unified support for UCS. Whilst most of us contributed money on a weekly basis, some didn't.

The image that sticks with me mostly is that of the yard gates opening up and people spewing out in their thousands. Vast numbers of people like bees out of a hive. You had to run and fight for a seat on the bus, lines and lines of buses. That's one of my earliest recollections. In some ways it's a common image, but for me it's an abiding image – the first person squeezing out that narrow gap in the gate as they open, and, on the other side, the security men trying to hold you back. That ritual was played out every night reinforcing the difference between us and them.

The launch, I think, was the other big image. A lot of people played launches down on the basis that if you'd seen one you'd seen them all – but there was a genuine collective sense of pride there. You'd get the view that it wasn't as good as the last one, and even yet, you've a lot of people building ships in pubs and clubs and old men's huts all over that area. But there is no doubting that there was a tremendous sense of pride in what could be a really brutal industry.

Willie Miller
Timekeeper, John Brown & Co Ltd

I started in John Brown's in October 1948. I came out of the Army in 1947 and went back to Singer's where I'd worked before. I left there and opened a wee sweet shop and closed it down again. There were vacancies in the yard. I saw the head timekeeper and it was a job as a timekeeper and I got a start. All of my family, my brothers and my father worked in Singer's, no-one had worked in shipbuilding.

I had to go out in the morning and check my men in. I had a little shed with a window and a board with two hundred slots and everybody had a check number on a wee metal disc with their number stamped on. You checked the men in by them calling their number to you and you gave them one of the discs as each man had two. You cleared up, marked your absentees and then took the box and sorted it for dinner time. You then had to write up your time books. And that was around the time that the biro came out. Before that it was pen and ink, so I was pleased to see the biro.

The books had spaces for the man's name, badge number and for jobs and times for his jobs and that tied up with the man's total hours and overtime. On the Wednesday you took your book in and that went through the head timekeeper, the foreman signed it and that book then went up to the gatehouse for payment and the man's rates were at the bottom of the page – all the premium hours, regular hours and overtime hours.

The piecework system was more complicated. Mind you, it was piecework of sorts and there was a blind eye turned to some of it. If you were getting say 6/6d an hour, you were getting that money but it changed if the foreman gave you a job and then he said you'd done a particularly good job he would boost them up. Give them an extra 1d an hour or so and he would authorise that by giving me a slip to put into the man's sheet.

That went on for a while and I then did a spell in the joiners', which at some times was the biggest joiners' shop in

Britain and I then went to the platers' shop and they were the boys that built the ships. I was in the caulking department for a while and there were machine caulkers and hand caulkers.

There was a section there with acetelyne burners and you went onto the boat with a paint pot of a specific colour and you said to the lad, what did you do today? and he would show you. I painted the work, marking off so many feet of beams or girders or whatever it was, marked down the amount of footage, went back to the office, looked up the rate sheets and costed it against what the man had done.

One of the really awful things was sacking people. The Head of Affairs came to me one day, and they could be really ruthless, and he said to me, Willie, there were so many men discharged last Friday, you've got fourteen timekeepers and you only need twelve. You've got to sack two, tell me who they are.

So as it happened there were two of them off sick. Wee Peter, who'd lost his legs on one of the ships, was lying up in Gartnaval Hospital. He had bother with his stumps, and the other lad was Maxy, he was a blacksmiths' timekeeper and he had a bad bout of the 'flu or something. I had to go up and tell them about it that Friday and I even had to lie to get into the hospital. I had to say that I had good news for a patient, it was a sin. So I walked in and wee Peter was lying in bed and he was a great wee guy, and when I came in he said, I know what you've come up for, I've been waiting on you coming through that door but don't worry about it Willie.

I went from there to see Maxy and he was lying in bed and he said, I know what you've come for, don't worry about it. I've said to the wife, Willie will be up any minute. The men were taking the heat off of me but it was a bad thing.

I finished in October 1986. The one thing that sticks in my mind is the men, rough diamonds, but they were all good men.

Tony Mitchell
Ship's draughtsman, Fairfield Shipbuilding & Engineering Co Ltd

I grew up in London but had a very romantic idea about Scotland and ships. I had a choice of Fairfield's or a yard on the south coast. I chose Fairfield's. And it worked. I was there for just under forty years. I had an uncle who was in ship repair, he was a Glaswegian. When he heard that I was going into ship-building he wrote to my father and said, the boy's nuts, it's a dying industry. That was in the late 1950s.

I can still remember my first day very clearly, walking up the stairs in the turret, as they called it, at the back of the drawing office and going and standing outside the assistant chief's office. Standing there, trying to understand what the other boys around me were talking about, just getting the accent right. I was lucky, they were very good to me. Very mixed group of people, it was good fun. I settled in fairly quickly. Got used to the ribbing, learnt to give it back. Think I'm naturalised now.

I served an apprenticeship as a draughtsman on the ship side. The bit I started in was the side of shipbuilding that deals with people onboard. Not the steel work, but the way the ship works, the cargo, navigation, accommodation. I spent nearly all my time doing that.

All the other yards used to call Fairfield's the rest-home. It was quite easy going. As an apprentice it wasn't too difficult to skive if you wanted to. But it was interesting. You had to draw on tracing paper. Once you got better at it you got round to using linen and ink.

I remember in 1965 we had an announcement from the chief to say that the receiver was coming in. As a boy you don't really take too much interest. I was thoroughly enjoying myself. That was the start of it. The old Fairfield's closed and the marine engineering side Fairfield Rowan. Fairfield's Glasgow was formed, then Upper Clyde Shipbuilders then Govan Shipbuild-ers, then Kværner. So it was continual change.

I was a happy-go-lucky sort of bloke. Other places were closing all round us. Why Fairfield's continued, I've got my theories about that, but it was very strange that that yard, so far up river and not where you'd expect to find a large shipyard, and yet it continued. We stayed with medium size ships. The last tanker we built was *British Gas*, 60,000 tons, which was nothing. We were a versatile yard too.

I'd like to have seen the Fairfield Experiment go on a bit longer. It was full of great ideas. Some of them weren't going to work, but others had a good chance. It would have been good to see if they really could make a go of it. Upper Clyde Shipbuild-ers kept us in business however. The idea of having combined yards was OK, but it was always very difficult working one yard to another. The individual yards had their own method of doing things.

As far as work was concerned, when you got a new ship and an early general arrangement there were lots of things you could do, you could put things in, move things around, try and think about the way the thing worked, 200 scale, you can put a lot of thought into it. To me that was the best job, didn't come around too often. I enjoyed going into the yard, looking at things. My favourite department in the old days was the blacksmiths' shop – all these fires going everywhere, it was like a vision of hell. Of course in the winter it was always lovely and warm.

It was getting a bit stressed at the end. The workforce was getting smaller and smaller and all the systems were beginning to break down. You used to know exactly who you could turn to for information or to give a job to or ask advice from someone in the yard. You'd turn around and find, sorry, he left last week. You ended up shovelling work through without being able to give it what you felt was due consideration. It was getting pretty frantic. It's hard to believe it's eighteen months since I left.

Building ships is not like any other industry. You're building this large village, then you're going to push it down a slipway and it's going to float and deal with all the problems it's got out there. It was a wonderful industry to be in, so many interests in it. It's a crying shame.

Willie Motherwell
Foreman Loftsman, Harland & Wolff, Govan

My brother, who was a welder with the British Arc Welding Company on the ships, got in tow with the foreman shipwright at Harland and Wolff and talked him into giving me a job as an apprentice shipwright. That was in 1947. Me being a fifteen year-old, I couldn't go into the yard. I had to go elsewhere, so they put me into the loft. I loved it. I fairly took to the whole thing, lining off and developing plates etc, doing all the physical but technical stuff. It attracted me considerably and I became a kind of workaholic.

As it so happened, when I turned eighteen, I was exempt from being called up because I was in shipbuilding. The foreman took me in and said, Willie, I'm afraid you'll need to go out into the yard and serve the last of your time as a shipwright, climbing up and down ships. However that wasn't my kettle of fish, so I managed to talk my foreman into keeping me on in the loft until my time was up. So that was my vocation for the rest of my life. I reckon I must have been one of the first lads that served all his time as a loftsman in the Clyde, because it was a mandatory thing that you must do a couple of years round the yard to learn the system. But I didn't do that.

I wouldn't say they were ruthless but in those days the manager put the fear of God in you. He came over to me and the first thing he said was, What school did you go to? Lambhill Street Junior Secondary, I said. He just patted me on the shoulder, You'll do well, he said. You could get a Rangers player's autograph no bother if you worked in Harland & Wolff.

If you went for a job at Harland's, you turned up in the morning to a place that was known as The Market. It was in Water Row beside the plater's shed where the new houses are now. You would go at 7 in the morning, maybe 50 or 60 men. The foreman would come along and say you, you, not you, you, and so on. You were picked out to work. If your face fitted, you were in, That's the way they worked it. I wouldn't say it was a religious yard in the bitter sense. Let me put it this way, it was the way the foremen handled it. They didn't employ Catholics so they had no problems. There were Catholics of course, but they were there undercover.

I thought Harland's was a good yard. There was quite a close community about the place. They weren't very up-to-date in their equipment. I don't mean they were in the dark ages, but they had a good community of people. There was something a wee bit special about Harland & Wolff in Govan because we had that extra connection in Belfast. We probably got a share of any work that was going which was good for employment in Govan. But in those days it didn't matter too much as you could move about from yard to yard easily. If someone was paying you tuppence an hour more in the yard next door, you moved on there. If the situation changed, you could always come back.

I was sent over to Belfast three times with Jimmy Boyd, our production manager, to look at new cutting machines for the loft. We installed a Hancock cutting machine at Govan, a one-to-one machine that cut big templates. It showed you all the cut-outs and the shape of the ship. It was manual then, not like now with numerical control and computers, but I think we only had it installed about three months when the yard went into liquidation and closed down. That was 1963.

I started at Fairfield's. It was new technology with cutting machines and all the rest of it, a learning period. I was a year and a half in there when Jimmy McCallum, the foreman, called me in one day and said, I'm going away to Belfast. I said, fair enough. I was just a tenth-scale loftsman. He said, I'm recommending you for the foreman's job here. And that was me until I retired.

I enjoyed my work. It was hard work, very hard work. Guys were out there in the rain, the snow, and you didn't get time off. When the gaffer said work, you worked.

George O'Hara
Draughtsman, Charles Connell & Co Ltd

I joined Connell's in 1962 as an apprentice ship draughtsman and left in 1967. I went back into the industry in 1972 at Govan Shipbuilders, the old Fairfield yard, which was saved from the debacle of Upper Clyde Shipbuilders and spent two years there before going to Clydebank to work at John Brown Offshore at Rothesay Dock.

Even then shipbuilding on the Clyde was in decline. So, following the Geddes Report instituted by Harold Wilson, there was a serious attempt being made to retain the industry. The reorganisation, therefore, was for the right reasons but what was wrong was the way in which it was done. Everyone could see the value of shipbuilding to the economy especially around Clydeside. It supported steel, coal mining and transport quite apart from the ancillary industries that made the things that went into ships – cables, lights, all sorts of fittings, a huge range of things. Competition had become very intense and even in the 1950s things began to get tight. On the Clyde the firms responded by spending what were sizeable sums of money on modernisation. But the schemes never really went far enough and when profits dried up in the late 1950s and early 1960s so did the modernisation. The customer base was also narrowing. Lots of shipping companies traded with Britain's former colonies and they developed their own shipping companies, so they didn't want the Harrison Line or the Elder Line. The nature of shipping was also changing with the traditional trades being attacked by containerisation. So despite the fact that the order book was good the profits were small. The whole idea of UCS therefore, was to try and turn the tide.

The problem was that the five companies which constituted UCS had been historically in competition with each other. With the exception of Connell's, which was a pure merchant yard, all the other yards, for example, competed for naval orders. They all built merchant ships so were in competition there too. The way it turned out was an unmitigated disaster and lasted less than three years. The ships were late and few made any profit. When UCS collapsed, Rolls Royce went down at the same time and the linkage between the two did create a certain groundswell of public opinion because both companies did have big order books.

The guys put up a magnificent campaign in terms of retaining the industry. I feel it's a pity that they weren't more critical of the management prior to the collapse as it was an open secret that the company was trading illegally. It was the sub-contractors and suppliers who wanted their bills paid but what does that say about the management? They say it was the creditors who forced UCS into liquidation but it hardly reflects well on the management. Where I think the attempt to turn the industry around failed abysmally was that the whole thing became a political contest between ideological right and ideological left. You had a so-called socialist government taking on a capitalist industry, using the public purse to taunt the shipbuilders for their failure to run the industry. An absolute nonsense!

All of this eroded the customer basis, you could just see it evaporate. Without customers where does an industry go? This wasn't helped by, dare I say it, the incompetence of those who were put into run the industry after Geddes. They did not have anything like the singular business ethos of the men that they were replacing. This is not slanderous, it's a fact. They failed to address the situation of rising wages and declining productivity. The industry could not be sustained on the basis of tens of thousands of men organised around craft lines. The major failure of the industry was the failure to move from a craft-based industry to one based on production engineering.

Whether the value of the industry was appreciated by the labour force *en masse* is highly debatable but I certainly feel that my character was formed there. I spent seven or eight years in shipbuilding and gained skill levels that sustained my working life. I worked with some great guys and see the whole thing as a personal debt.

Joe O'Rourke
Plater, Lithgow's Ltd

I started in 1966 as a boy in the joiner's shop down in the Kingston yard and I started my apprenticeship in March 1967 as a plater. I then went to Lamont's yard and was in there for five years. During that time I got involved in the trade union side. First of all I was the plater's shop steward and then convenor when the previous convenor got sacked for calling one of the management 'buster'. We were out on strike for five weeks but got nowhere and I took over as convenor.

The same thing befell me. I got into an affray with a foreman who sent a guy home for drinking. The trouble was that the foreman had been drinking along with the guy and had then sent him home. I had an argument with him over it and one word followed another and, to be fair, I did threaten him. So I got the bag for gross industrial misconduct – threatening a foreman. I did admit that I'd threatened him and said that I was wrong, that I should have stuck one on him right on the spot and at least got the satisfaction out of it. So the boys all wanted to go on strike but I said I was totally in the wrong and that I was off.

Eventually I got back into Scott Lithgow where I ended up as the platers' steward. In the steward's office there was a formica table and folk would sit there with a pencil and doodle on it and then just rub it off. We were in the board room at a meeting and wee Pat writes, Fuck Belch on the table although this is veneer not formica. So Pat nudges me because Belch is at the meeting – so I'm in despair. The following morning I'm in the steward's office and the phone goes and it's Belch who demands to see Pat. So up we go, Pat would only have been about twenty-three or so. You have to understand that guys were writing Fuck Belch all over the yard – it was on bulkheads, plates, walls, every-where, but the boardroom table was a different thing altogether. I thought we'd get the jail, never mind the bag, but to be fair, Pat apologised and I think his age got him away with it, although Belch was fuming and God knows what it cost to get the table sorted out. Notorious days.

Looking back though, you couldn't have foreseen that the river would decline in the way that it did. At the time of nationalisation there were thirteen thousand folk in Scott Lithgow and that wasn't counting what was on the periphery. At that time they were taking three or four hundred apprentices a year which was over seventy per cent of all school leavers in the catchment area.

On reflection, we did all sorts of things that we should never have done, fought for guys that we should never have fought for. There was a lot of lazy guys, guys that would stand in the toilet for three days telling a story, professional story tellers, very good at it. So out of the thirteen thousand we were probably carrying about three thousand professional wasters, who were incapable of, or too lazy to do the job. But I never thought it would reach the stage that it's at now.

Thatcher didn't want shipbuilding and it was just driven down and down. Basically we did contribute to it but not as much as people think. There was no respect in the situation.

If Ross Belch made a decision then it carried the stamp of infinite wisdom. It couldn't be challenged. For example he diluted labour. You had guys who were bus drivers, worked in the Co-op, whatever, brought in as platers, and in honest truth it was raining caulkers' tools, the place was a death trap. He took the simple view that if the job was twice as big then you needed twice the workforce.

John Quigley
Marine engineer, John G Kincaid & Co Ltd

I started on the 12th of August 1964 in John G Kincaid's engine works in Greenock. I started as an apprentice and my first job was a dock store boy. At that time, Kincaid's was installing machinery in about eight or nine ships at the same time. So that store would have all the tools and the heavy duty stuff that was required to do the installation.

You'd maybe have four ships at Port Glasgow, one at the Greenock Dockyard, and ships outfitting up in Glasgow and even in the North East coast of England. I did that for some months and then started at the apprentice school, where there were about twenty of us. We were locked in a sort of cage. It would be against health and safety at work now, but as you can imagine, all sorts of pranks and tricks got played. We were all training to be marine engineers and you started off with a block, a solid block of steel, and they asked you to chisel it. So people would get hacked in really aggressively only to find out later that you had to file it square again. The more vicious you were with the chisel the more time you had to spend with the file. After that you drilled holes in it, fixed hex gauges in it and then had to file it out again. If you were good at it, you would find that the faster you went the more you would get to do, so there were all these psychological tricks played on you. It all seems rather basic now but it did give you a fundamental understanding of working with your hands. Eventually we went back into the main yards, some went to the turning, some to the fitting shop, others to the boiler shop and plumbers' shop.

I moved from Arthur Street, which did fabrications, valves and components – the boiler and plumbing shops were both there – to East Hamilton Street which had the finishing shops, the heavy machine shops and the assembly and test shops for the engines. So I had fifteen months in Arthur Street before moving and starting work in the finishing shop. After that I went to the test shop where the engines were tested and you would follow the engine after it was installed on the ship, go out on sea trials, take all the readings and check the efficiency of the engine. Just before I finished my time, I moved again to the installation department which actually put the engines into the ship. That meant that I worked in nearly all the yards on the river, from Ailsa at Troon all the way up to the big crane at Finnieston in Glasgow.

Initially conditions were pretty poor with us being sub-contractors, albeit long-established *bona fide* ones. But for facilities we tended to use boxes which equpment came in, turned over with tarpaulins pulled over them for shelters. That sort of situation went on until the late seventies. Around about the time of nationalisation you'd get a portacabin and conditions started to improve. If you were working in Glasgow, you'd get bused up in the morning and bused back in the evening and there were great arguments about the level of out-working allowance and the condition of the buses and such like. Mind you, some people would have gone to Glasgow on the back of a dust cart just to get the allowance.

When I started in Kincaid's they employed about eight hundred people. All it does now is spares for slow speed diesels. You knew things were getting steadily worse. We tended to limp along like twentieth century Long John Silvers, from one crisis to next. If the industry hadn't been nationalised it would have disappeared. From 1979 though, with Thatcher in power you had the attitude that nationalised industries were a bad thing *per se* and that shipbuilding was an antiquated, out of date, smokestack industry which should be gotten rid of.

In the eighties it was just one crisis after another with yards closing everywhere. I left Kincaid's in 1989 just after it was privatised. It stopped engine assembly in 1991.

Fred Reid
Assistant Chief Ship Surveyor, Lloyd's Register

I wanted to go to the cadet training college in Portsmouth at 15 but my parents refused, which was not surprising. It was the winter of 1942-43 and it was very severe winter. The outcome was that I became an apprentice shipbuilder, one of two in the Blythswood shipyard. I did a five year apprenticeship and on completion, I went to Barclay Curle to get experience in estimating. I then went back to Blythswood because the naval architect was retiring and I was given his job.

I started my career with Lloyds as a ship surveyor in 1955. It was an entirely different view of ships and shipbuilding. My first two years at Lloyds were spent in the plan approval office where all the classification plans were sent in from the various shipyards in Scotland and examined by us for approval.

At that time our yards were really made for riveted ships, and if a yard submitted a drawing with welded details, the strength of that welding was based on the riveted factor. But when I went to Sweden, the only riveting done there was in the repair yard, ships were built completely of welded construction.

In Sweden, one of the first things that impressed me was the attitude of the yard managers to the union. On one occasion, I had a serious problem only a few weeks into my career there. I requested an interview with the Managing Director on the Monday morning. I went to his office and his secretary said I'm sorry, he's in a meeting. I said, I'll wait for him. She said, I don't think you should wait, he'll be much longer than you'll want to wait, he's having his morning meeting with the unions. I had just come from the Clyde where a shipyard manager probably didn't want to be on the same side of the street as the union representative never mind have a Monday morning meeting with him. The other thing was that it was a much more modern yard, with a lot of equipment, welding machines and so on, which I hadn't seen before.

By the time I reached Belfast after my years in Sweden, Harland & Wolff were trying to introduce the welding machines there. The unions started off by arguing that this machine was going to do the work of five men, so they wanted five men to operate it. They reached the old British compromise, there would be a man to operate it, a man to set it up, and a labourer to stand by it, three men. This meant the shipbuilders were paying for new machinery which was operated at a very high cost to them with three men operating it instead of one.

Looking back, of course I went into shipbuilding in the Clyde with the belief that I was joining the best shipbuilders in the world, that Clyde-built was everything. I had no reason to doubt that at all.

When I went to John Brown's, I was very impressed by all that I saw. They were building a 44,000 ton tanker for Shell International. That was a mammoth ship in those days, I felt quite proud to be there and to be part of it. But when I went further afield it became clear we were not advancing in the way that others were.

There is no doubt that the Clyde before and during the war, had an excellent reputation. But it never advanced the way shipbuilding in the Far East advanced after the end of the war. I can't think of any new technology that was tried on the Clyde or in Britain in fact, most of it came from elsewhere.

But it doesn't excuse the ignorance of what was going on in the rest of the world. They must have been blind not to see what the Japanese were doing and that the Swedes were building mammoth tankers in such a short space of time. Not only building them but telling you the day the keel was going to be laid, the day the ship was going to be floated out and the day it was going to be handed over.

Jimmy Reid
Fitter, John Brown & Co Ltd

Given that I was a fitter I was in and out of a lot of the yards on the river – Stephen's, Fairfield's, and Clydebank. But that wasn't all that unusual. I can remember going to Clydebank and feeling a sense of incredulity. The yard had a huge reputation and they had built many of the great Cunarders. But when you went into the place you had to ask how these sophisticated ships had been built when the technology was, in many ways, turn of the century stuff. There was a crudeness about it. Sure there had been investment here and there, but they had built all these technologically sophisticated vessels and you just marvelled at it given the available technology. It was almost like a Fred Flintstone building.

Despite the fact that there was investment in the British shipbuilding industry it was too little and it was too late. I don't subscribe to the view that it was bad management, bad working practices or bad workers. This was the same management and workers who had ruled the world before the First World War and even after the Second War. The Clyde, which is a wee river, had launched a ridiculously high percentage of world tonnage throughout the modern era. I am certain that when they did try to repair the damage of under-investment it was too late. That was when a certain incompetence and dogma came to the fore. These virtually sacrificed the industry, but the basic cause was the lack of investment.

I can speak from experience as I was there at the time. There were two factors to bear in mind. First of all, the nature of industrial relations in the industry were strongly shaped by how the industry was run. What I mean by this is that it was recognised that when a ship was launched and finished you got the sack. So when there was a pool of unemployment you would have the situation of men expediting the completion of a ship, which meant their dismissal. When you moved into the full-employment conditions of the post-1945 period this was a crazy way to run an industry. Where was the incentive to produce when you asked people to speed their work to a

conclusion only to get the sack? Even in UCS when we had a lot of orders and no employment worries, we could have shifted people about the yards and cracked that particular nut. But even then, I was conscious that there was a profound psychological factor in all of this. That workers would attempt to exploit good market conditions to enhance their wages is not to be marvelled at, it was totally rational.

Second, it was really a bit hard to take from people who preached the loss of the market – the same people who were building ships in a seller's market and who would screw that market – who seemed to think that labour had no right to maximise their own return. What had happened historically was that a division of labour by trade had developed, rational enough in its time, but which suited employers in that they played the unions off against each other. The public were given the impression that this was all trade union militancy, but it wasn't.

At one stage you had thirty different unions in the shipbuilding industry and these circumstances spawned a ridiculous situation. Instead of facing one set of negotiations over wages and making some sense of the rates, they would negotiate by department. So the welders would go in one week and negotiate something and the platers would say, hang on a minute, and they would go in the next week and then it would be the electricians and so forth and so on. So you'd get disputes – one week it would be the caulkers, that would bugger up production, then it would be the electricians and so it would go on. But what was a logical division of labour in say 1890 was farcical in the 1950s; it was a fragmentation of labour deeply rooted in history. It was a much more complex thing than was generally recognised and the bottom line was that we had not moved on.

There was a complete lack of imagination on both sides. It was a wee change here, a wee change there, but that was useless in that what was coming was an absolute revolution.

Willie Robb
Welder, Lithgow's Ltd

I left school in 1949 on a Friday afternoon and was taken up to what became Scott Lithgow's East Yard – it was Lithgow's at the time – on the Saturday and told to come back on the Monday morning. I started my apprenticeship as a welder and I worked in there for twenty seven years. I had two years of broken service for National Service between 1954 and 1956 and when I went back to the yard I'd become interested in the trade union movement and I became firstly, the welders' shop steward and then the yard convenor. I was elected to the West of Scotland District Committee and served on that for twelve years, with nine as Chairman. From there I was elected by the membership in the West of Scotland and Ayrshire as a full time official of what was then the Boilermaker's Society.

We've moved on since then as far as the unions are concerned. We amalgamated with the GMW and today we're known as the GMB. I retired in September 1998 and that's pretty much my working life. My first wage in the yard in 1949 was 19/1d, old money, and that was working a forty-seven hour week. My first piece-work pay, and you didn't get that until you were into your second year, was £2.5s, so there was slow grinding progress. My recollection is that your wages were made up solely of overtime. It became part and parcel of your working life, two nights and a Saturday.

When I started, the majority of the workforce was riveters and the welding had just started to creep in. It was a new concept in shipbuilding and as welding techniques progressed, there was the demise of riveted ships, so much so that welding became the predominant mode of production. In 1949 most of the shell of the ship was still riveted. You'd have the odd butt and stuff like that but as it progressed you had what became known as fabrication, a great American system, constructing small units in the fabrication sheds which would then be taken out and put on the boat, followed by fairing up, burning, and a welder would come along and weld up the butts, so much so that the riveting squads got cut back and it was a really rapid process. From an all-riveted ship to an all-welded ship seemed to take no time at all.

I didn't have a real sense of crisis in the industry until the 1960s. There were one or two yards in difficulties, a few closures, but I suppose UCS marked the first real crisis and although there was a magnificent effort by the working class movement to keep these yards open, things were uncertain from then on.

I had a grandfather who worked in Harland and Wolff's and an uncle who was a riveter in Lithgow's. They used to start at six in the morning and have their breakfast at eight and then go back to work. So the family was connected to the industry as most families in the area were in one way or another. I liked the job, mostly because I didn't know any better, but I did enjoy it. There were a lot of good people in the industry on both sides. I met a lot of nice people in the industry and made some good friends there too. Greenock was shipbuilding, marine engineering and sugar. Now there's next to nothing, there's little left and it's all rather sad.

I remember when I first went in as an apprentice there were no toilets and you had to go below the boat and eventually they got a big trough somewhere and put a tin roof on it and that constituted progress and modernisation. It was the uncertainty of the industry that created the demarcation barriers but when you looked at it in the wider context it was the wrong attitude because it was a hold-up in the yards. Demarcation originated to save jobs but maybe in the end it cost jobs.

Bill Scott
Engineer/draughtsman, Fairfield Shipbuilding & Engineering Co Ltd

I started, I remember it clearly, on the 4th of August 1958, as an apprentice engineer in what was then the Fairfield Shipbuilding and Engineering Company. I ended up finishing my apprenticeship as a jig and tool design draughtsman in the Works Department of the Engine Shop.

These were great times for the Clyde although I wasn't really aware of that then. I would get some of the shipbuilding lore from my father who was the turbine foreman in Stephen's yard next door. That was why I started in Fairfield's because there was no way I was going to work with my old man. He didn't want me in shipbuilding at all. He saw it as a very, very hard life. He had served his apprenticeship in the depression years and worked one week and was off the next. During the war, he would often disappear on ship trials and he couldn't even tell my mother. Essentially, he worked his life away.

I left the business for a while and when I came back I joined the Govan Division of what was by then Upper Clyde Shipbuilders, having spent a year working in the Planning Department of Alexander Stephen's. I went to Govan as an Industrial Engineer, worked through that over a period of about three years and then took the position of Services General Manager for UCS.

Looking back, UCS is a very difficult one to judge. It's easy to say that it was wrong but without it – it's a bit like nationalisation – if it hadn't happened at the time it happened we would have had nothing left. What we've got now is the product of UCS. UCS itself was a very public event. Put it this way, the profile that the public got was not what was happening behind the scenes. The impression was that Jimmy Airlie and Jimmy Reid were running the yards and that's not strictly true, they were not. What they were doing was fighting to enable the yards to continue. UCS, initially, was far too big, there were too many diverse elements in it and the management set up headquarters which were very distant from the yards. They had a lot of good ideas but they wanted them all implemented everywhere at the same time.

Shipyards are very strange things, they've all got their own personality. You don't go to two different shipyards and find that they've got the same facilities – they'll have different berths, cranage, the layouts will be entirely different and constraints that will stop you building ships of a different size. Two feet on the beam, for example, can make or break tendering for an order.

A lot of yards were designed in different eras so facilities are very varied and you can't really say everyone will do it this way and put down very narrow and very rigid guidelines. I think that British Shipbuilders fell into this trap. There was a lot of imposition in UCS and British Shipbuilders. People are also different. There may be great similarities between the working guy on the shop floor at Govan and on the Tyne but they're not the same and the one thing I've found is that rivers divide communities.

Much of the problem, across British industry was about complacency – grey beards in the boardrooms. Shipbuilding had become a much more sophisticated industry – we looked on manufacturing as where we were in the world of the 1950s, 60s and 70s – complacency again.

Japan, Korea and others were looking at where they wanted to go. We had become small players by the end of the 1970s having lost huge market share in just twenty years. You don't just lose that sort of share, it almost has to be worked at to achieve it. It is an indictment of this industry. The culture, for which the only word was 'macho', has also changed a lot. For example, there would be very few wives who would have had a clue what their husband's earnings were if they worked in a shipyard. If someone got taken into hospital injured, the main concern, as likely as not, was to ensure that the wife didn't find a wage slip in a jacket pocket. Outside of Fairfield's on a Friday night, it looked as if there had ten weddings as thousands of wage slips got turned into confetti.

Davy Smart
Draughtsman, A& J Inglis & Co Ltd

I started in A&J Inglis's shipyard at Pointhouse on the north side of he river opposite the Harland and Wolff yard at Govan in 1954. I went in as an office boy, then went into the drawing office as an apprentice draughtsman. I worked in there until 1960 when I went to Connell's yard at Scotstoun. I was in Connell's until early 1964 and then I moved over the river into Fairfield's.

Once you were in Inglis's yard as the office boy and had done your stint there you could go to any department in the yard. I always fancied the drawing office. At that time I went to night school at Glasgow High. There was no day release, so you'd go to night school for three nights a week. It was a case of in from the work, a quick tea, and out again. Latterly you were offered some day release, one day a week at Paisley College. There were different things each night, naval architecture, applied mechanics and mathematics leading to the Ordinary National Certificate or your Higher National Certificate. So I did five years at night school until my time was out. Even when I was at Connell's I still went on for a further year. I got married then and that spoilt things!

Inglis at the time only built Admiralty tugs and small Irish coastal boats. I don't think that they were even two hundred feet long, so the ships were small. It was a good place to serve your time as you got well looked after. There weren't more than ten people in the drawing office so you could get a real variety of jobs – arrangement work, piping work, steelwork drawings and so on. Inglis launched their boats into the River Kelvin and they were so small that they very seldom needed to sail into the Clyde.

I don't suppose there would have been more than four or five hundred people in the yard at any given time. It was a bit daunting when I went to Connell's, all of a sudden you were hit with huge bulkhead drawings for a big tanker. I panicked and wanted to run out the door but again you were well looked after.

The money was fairly poor in Inglis and Connell's were offering a few pounds more which was a big difference then. When I moved from Connell's to Fairfield's it was for an extra ten shillings a week. At that time I was getting thirteen pounds which was the union rate and that was a big difference. For instance, sometimes when we finished work at Connell's there were five of us who used to go for a pint and you'd get change from ten shillings.

I was there at the time of the Fairfield Experiment and went through all the crises. The company name was Fairfield, Fairfield Rowan, Fairfield (Glasgow), then the Govan Division of Upper Clyde Shipbuilders, Govan Shipbuilders and then finally Kværner Govan. I was involved in the UCS work-in and it seemed to go from one crisis to another but you didn't really think that it could all come to an end. It seemed inconceivable that it could all end.

Mind you, the real crisis was the first one when the chief draughtsman called us all in on a Friday afternoon and said there was no money in the bank. That was a crisis! I suppose there have been so many industrial tragedies elsewhere.

It was a great job. There wasn't a day when I went in that I ever hated it, especially in the last ten years when the computers came in. I had to get re-trained and I was really slow, all the young lads were passing me by, but then I mastered it and really loved it. So it was throw away the pencil and suddenly you had your own work station. You logged on, got your drawing on screen and got on with it. It was great, all these years on the board and then the CADCAM machines totally transformed your job.

Sandy Stephen
Director, Alexander Stephen & Co Ltd

I joined the company in 1951 after I had been in the navy and at university. My father tried to persuade me to go and work in some sensible industry. He said if you come into shipbuilding, you'll have nothing but trouble with trade unions and money. If you want a happy life, go and work somewhere else. I had always felt that I wanted to be a shipbuilder, and I was quite honestly appalled that he should even think of my wanting to do anything else. So I became a shipbuilder. But he was right, we did have nothing but trouble, but not for quite a few years.

There was an enormous sense of trust during the 1950s. We had our favourite owners and they had their favourite shipyards. We got on very well together. Mind you, they hadn't got much option because they accepted cost-plus ships, and they were pleased to get them. A ship to them meant they could make a huge amount of money. As long as they got their ships on time, they were very happy. That was the struggle we had. Shortage of steel, shortage of material made it very difficult.

Financially, the 50s were pretty good, but it was then that the seeds of destruction were sown, because it was quite clear the Japanese were coming up. When we saw their prices, we first of all assumed they were building rubbish, but in fact we very soon realised that they could build good ships at three-quarters the price of ours. It seemed the biggest threat in the 50s, was from the unions, but as people said, we've had these unions for a hundred years, so perhaps we can get by with them for another hundred. However, they were very wrong on that score. But it was very relaxed. There was a very good atmosphere, truly a sense of spirit. People joined the company and they tended to stay for life. There were a few people who moved around, but your long service people were really loyal. We employed about 4,000 people. We were up to 5,000 after the war when we were converting ships back to merchant use. Then we dropped to about 3,500 in the mid 1960s. That includes the ship repair and the engineering side as well.

By 1963, I was absolutely convinced that we could go no further. I could see no way out for this industry because there was absolutely no give on the labour side. We could not get any extra productivity, in fact, productivity went up very little between 1945 and the 1960s, virtually no increase, because the unions wanted to have all the advantages. It was a very depressing time when one had to encourage other people to work and become more efficient, whereas in your heart of hearts you knew you were battering your head against a brick wall. We'd had our time, and it's very difficult when you start declining to arrest it and get back up again.

In the 1950s we were leading the country on pre-fabrication. My uncle John organised that the boilermakers and the shipwrights should work together in a combined team to erect parts of the ship. It was working very well until the next shipyard came along wanting to do the same thing. Both unions, shipwrights and the boilermakers, realised that there was a risk of their losing out to the other and so our yard became a battleground for the British shipbuilding industry. There was a demarcation strike which lasted for six months. It very nearly bankrupted the company. After that we did not feel like leading the field again.

I have to admit as a young man I was sometimes appalled by the attitudes of some of the other shipbuilders. Some of them had an amazing attitude, they would not give an inch on anything. But these attitudes go back for a hundred or more years. There was always a them and us. In my great great great grandfather's diary, you read about his troubles in Aberdeen when he was building ships there. His labour relations were very good, but there were still strikes, there was still trouble. This attitude persisted right through. The employers allowed flexibility to disappear completely when they had bonus rates and when they started building iron ships. We were landed with such demarcation that we could not do anything about it unless there was a national change. That didn't happen in shipbuilding. I was very pleased to be out of the place.

Ian Sutherland
Plater/draughtsman, Yarrow Shipbuilders Ltd

I started out as a plater. That was in 1977. I left school at 16 and went into Yarrow's. I knew there was a few places to apply for apprenticeships. Yarrow's was one, Govan Shipbuilders and Barr & Stroud, were others. I've been here ever since.

It's a bit like being at school. You're treated like kids. Management treat us like big kids. It's an us and them thing. It still is that way. It definitely was when I first went in. When I first went in it was a nationalised company and it went from being nationalised to being a private company – Yarrow's, then GEC, now it's Marconi. It's probably going to be British Aerospace soon.

There's a good camaraderie among the workforce. But morale isn't very high at all. I think there's a possibility the place is going to close. They can see a lot of the faults, and a lot of things that could be put right. We just feel that it could be us at some point. It's just life in the shipyards as far as we're concerned, it's been like that ever since we've been working there.

I think it will get to the point when there's only one or two shipyards in the country. We're almost there now. There's only Barrow and what's left on the Clyde. That's it.

Two months ago I just started working as a draughtsman, which is quite good because there are more possibilities as a draughtsman. There are a lot of avenues open now that weren't before. Once you're a plater, there's a chance you'd be that all your life.

I heard my Dad saying that when he saw a ship being launched, he felt it was a bit of him going away. I don't know if it's a generation thing, but I don't feel that at all. To me it's just a job. I don't think there's the same fulfilment that my Dad seems to have had from his work. It's just somewhere you go to earn money. A lot of the pure enjoyment of work has been taken away. I think it's because things have become more automated. It's like a production line. You do a certain amount of work, every day you go in you do a certain amount, and it's the same thing that you do every day.

I don't think I'll get a lifetime out of shipbuilding like my Dad. To be honest I don't think so.

(Ian Sutherland is the son of James Sutherland p108/109)

James Sutherland
Welder, John Brown & Co Ltd

I started an apprenticeship in 1945 at John Brown's and was there up to the time of Marathon and UIE. I actually came from the north of Scotland, Wick, to get a job. I was amazed at shipbuilding. It was a complete change from the north of Scotland.

In the 50s and 60s, things were especially busy. At that time there was plenty of work in all the yards, that people used to go from one yard to another, They'd get fed up and say I'll just take my books and start somewhere else. It was quite easy.

At night when the horn went, there was just a stampede to get out the gate. It was ten past five you stopped at night, then Singer's came out at the same time, it was chock-a-block. The trams couldn't cope with them. We used to jump on lorries, used to chap on the cabin when you wanted to get off. They'd put the bunnet round and everybody would put money in it and give it to the driver.

There were cruel streaks in some of the foremen. There was one, I can't remember his name, but he was a 'hatman'. A bowler hat man. He used to go into the shed where the apprentices boiled the cans for the journeymen's tea. They'd get half a crown a week for boiling up. There's was this big furnace. You nipped down there about ten minutes before the horn and try and boil the cans at the furnace. Someone would look out for the 'hatman', and if he was spotted, you ran away. He'd open the furnace door, and of course, with that terrific heat, the cans melted. You'd to buy new cans. They didn't do it every time. Some days they'd just kick the cans over.

There's maybe twelve to fourteen welds in a tank, and within half an hour you couldn't see in front of you because of the fumes. You'd to come out to get some fresh air, a quarter hour break then you were back in again. It never cleared. There were big fans, but they weren't effective enough to cope with it. It was just a big fan stuck onto the top of the tank to draw the fumes out the best it could.

I was quite proud to see some of the ships being built. Especially the *QE2*. I welded on her shell. Beautiful ship, one of the finest ships to be built in the yard. It was part of my life going down that river.

I didn't expect John Brown to ever close. I thought they'd be the last yard on the Clyde to close to be honest, because of the reputation they had. Very sorry to see it close, very sad.

I'm six years retired now. I enjoyed my time. I liked it, I really liked my work. I would start over again, I wouldn't miss anything. Just got memories now. Good memories.

Alex Wilson
Engineer, John G Kincaid & Co Ltd

I started in Kincaid's in September 1964 coming straight from school into the time office.

I worked there for a year and then went to the training school in our other premises down in Arthur Street. After my year in the training school I was allocated a department to go to defined by trade. I was an engineer but you also had boilermakers and such like in the place. I went to East Hamilton Street where I finished my apprenticeship. Everybody that worked at Kincaid's tended to have somebody in their family who was working there, a dad, uncle, brother, whatever. My dad worked all his days in Kincaid's and I had a brother there as well although he was made redundant in 1990, but it was basically a very big firm for family connections, fathers to sons.

When I started, the company employed about eight hundred in the factory space but we had a full-time outside squad, fitters, who actually installed the engines in the ships so there were a few hundred in that. There was also an outside squad on Tyneside so there would be upwards of twelve hundred working there at any one time. My basic task as an engineer was as a turner, although I didn't do a lot of lathe work which most folk would identity with turning. I always worked on horizontal and vertical boring on the larger types of machinery. We had the light machine shop, small lathes, banks and banks of them, the other departments were medium to heavy, some of the larger components for the engines, the bed plate, the crankshaft, for example. You weren't talking a couple of tons, you were talking a couple of hundred tons. I was in the heavy machine shop and I worked on the crankshafts, bed plates, main engine frames, all the heavy parts of the engine.

It was really well into the 1970s before I really had any sense that the industry was running into difficulties and then it seemed to go from bad to worse. As you look out the door some nights you think, that used to be our prefabrication shop, now it's a hamburger shop, and our major works is just rubble now.

During the early days of the redundancies it was quite incredible how they did it. Everybody stood by their machine at one o'clock and they came round with letters and if you got one, that was you off. If you didn't then you still had a job for a time. So you were cowering. I remember one day, there were twenty of us in this section and by the end of the day there were only two left. I'm fifty one years of age and I'm probably the third oldest person working for the company. The last time we started an apprentice was about five years ago and even then it was only two, compared to about thirty or forty a year when I started.

For a long while there were shipping company representatives in the works and if any of the lads fancied going to sea as engineers then it was almost as simple as knocking on the door of say, Denholm's, and you were in. But, of course, with the decline of the British merchant marine that all ended as well.

Not long after Kværner took over we were all summoned to a mass meeting where the guy stood in front of six hundred of us and unveiled the business plan which gave us a year to get the thing turned around. They posted redundancy notices four weeks later for three hundred people. So from being guaranteed a year, the workforce was halved in a month and from 1989 to 1991 we went from six hundred down to ninety employees.

I'd have to say that there must be a future for this industry, it's the only thing that I know how to do. I wouldn't even know how to go and sign on the brew. Look at the jobs that are being created, call centres for example, they'd be totally alien to anyone who's worked in this industry or probably not even achievable as lots of us don't have keyboard skills.

Jan Wilson
Secretary, Kværner Govan Ltd

I left school at 17 when a job came in and I just applied for it basically. The yard was only minutes from where I lived. I stayed in a 'four in a block' house, and the girl downstairs from me worked in the yard, even my first kitten came from the yard.

It was a job in a typing pool with lots of girls, about thirty typists, and also a load of girls who were comptometer operators. A lot more staff then than there is now. At that time very few managers had their own secretaries, no-one had their individual assistants. We all sat in a pool and you went to departments as needed.

Because you were in the office, you didn't have much to do with production, so you could be in the main office for a long time and not be at all concerned with what was going on in the yard. Once in a blue moon you'd go down to the yard to see a ship being launched. There were loads and loads of people cheering, not that we don't get that now. But at the moment they're a wee bit disinclined to cheer.

When I started in here I was one of the quietest wee souls. Now I can stand up to anyone, my mouth goes before my brains get in gear. You get like the people in here. You get to be sharp. When the Norwegians came in, it was frightening at first, because you had to think twice before you said anything. That was because they didn't understand our sense of humour.

They were different people, different natures. We always like to laugh, he'd say. Because I'm laughing do you think I'm not working? They kept coming round and talking about our culture, the difference in culture, because it is quite different.

I started in the typing pool, as I said, and then moved to the electrical drawing office. I worked in there for some time and then I left. I came back five years later into the Maintenance Department, and worked there for another eighteen years.

Then, eight years ago, they started cutting back drastically. Kværner had got the yard by then and they were cutting back. A lot of people were leaving, redundancies were coming up so I had to leave the Maintenance Department and be the secretary to the Production Director, because they couldn't afford a secretary in both areas.

This is the worst crisis there has been, most definitely. Before, we were owned by British Shipbuilders, and it was said that we were spending money that we didn't have, we were well over budget. Now we're a private company and private companies need to make money. At present we're finding it really difficult. It's not that our people aren't working hard, they're very committed. The production workers are very committed, because there aren't the jobs outside that they would have expected before.

So this is the worst crisis there has been. We're all worried, but Jamie, our convenor, is keeping morale as high as he can, he's brilliant, he's doing very well. But yes, morale is low. Just now, we're waiting for word from the Kværner Chief Exec on what's happening to the Kværner Group itself, so we don't know what's going to happen to us. They could close us, we could be bought over, I don't know. It's very worrying, that's all I'll say.

Joyce upstairs has been here about thirty years, much the same as myself, and she's here because she enjoys it. There's not a lot of women left in the yard. Two in personnel, one assistant and one secretary, we've got Lynn and Ellen, myself and Moira, Joyce and Christine. I like it, and I like working with men. It's not a sexist thing, it's just that they're easier to deal with than working with women. If you fall out with them they still talk to you the next day.

Duncan Winning OBE
Engine draughtsman, John G Kincaid & Co Ltd

Basically, I didn't work with shipbuilders. I worked with the engine builders, Kincaid & Co of Greenock. They didn't just build engines, they did outfitting as well. By far most of their work was done with Scott's although they also worked with some of the yards up the river. I started my time as an apprentice fitter, sat the drawing office exam, became a draughtsman, moved from there into automation when that came into the shipyards, became what we call an instrumentation engineer, then a project engineer and finally drawing office administrator. That was the position I was in when I left the industry.

My father worked in Kincaid's. He was a foreman turner and subsequently became the apprentice supervisor, and on my mother's side of the family I have an uncle who was a manager in John Brown's. His son was involved in John Brown's as well in the gear fitting, he was a gear-fitting expert. So I have several family connections with shipbuilding.

On the lower reaches there was Scott's, and at that time the Greenock Dockyard was independent. There was also 'Siberia', as it was known, George Brown's in Greenock, then up to Port Glasgow and Lithgow's and Hamilton's, and of course a whole host of yards up the river.

When I joined Kincaid, the last steam engine they ever built, a triple expansion, was sitting ready to be stripped down and sent out. We built, mainly Burmeister and Wain, that was the main licence through most of my time, but as British Shipbuilders contracted, after we were nationalised, we ended up being the last engine builder in the UK. We inherited all the drawings from the other engine builders to supply spares, and we also inherited the licences to build other engines, so towards the end we were also building Sulzer high and medium speed engines.

But then we had a long history of building steam engines, which were all designed in-house. We also built boilers, mainly Scotch boilers, but I believe, before my time, they did water tube boilers. We did a lot of installation work of other people's engines. The big steam tankers that Lithgow's built, for instance, had Stal Laval turbines. We didn't just install the engines in their ships, we purchased all the engine auxiliaries. We provided the propeller, we provided the funnel, the only thing in the engine we didn't do was the domestic plumbing and salt water pumps.

The really bad times were when we got involved in the big orders from the Maritime Fruit Company. When they crashed they had placed such a tremendous number of orders that it made a big dent in the industry, and the government of the day was not sympathetic to shipbuilding. Some of the comments from Government either showed ignorance of the industry, naivety or downright antagonism. You can take your pick which of these three you want. There were problems with unions, but it was not all one-sided. I know of quite a number of disputes that did not arise from the unions, they were actually engineered by management for different commercial advantages at the time.

Some things never really reached the press. You have to realise that if a ship owner doesn't have any work or contracts for a ship, they'll do everything to delay its delivery from the builders because they don't want to accept the expense of operating it. The Greek ship owners were very good at that. They didn't have a contract for the first of these super-tankers that we built. A ship is like a small town. Nothing in a small town has everything working perfectly at the one time, there's always a problem somewhere, a light- fitting slightly squint and so on. So you can always find something on the ship that is not right.

There was an awful lot of things going on behind the scenes by people that had made their minds up, for whatever reason, that shipbuilding had to go, but I think what was also not appreciated, was that shipbuilding was merely the end product of a whole line of manufacturing. It was merely the box that contained lots of other people's products.

Sir Eric Yarrow
Managing Director, Yarrow Shipbuilders Ltd

Yarrow's has been a public company since 1920 so we were really the odd man out as far as family firms were concerned; there were Scott's, Lithgow's, Denny's Connell's and Stephen's and so on, largely owned by families, but we were a public company.

My holding in Yarrow's was one and a half per cent and if you looked at all the relatives I suppose we would have got up to about fifteen per cent at the most, so we were a very different company from most on the Clyde. In fact, we prided ourselves on our labour relations in Yarrow's and took a lot of trouble over working relations. On one occasion a personnel manager came to see me and said that we had an undesirable plumber in the yard and that we might have some trouble strike-wise. I said 'strike' and he said to me that I'd better come along to the meeting. So I went along to the meeting, never met the chap before, and he said to me, 'how are you Eric?' and I said, 'how are you Jock?' and he said we've got a little bit of a dispute here but you own the place so all you have to do is sign on the line, and I said to him, 'my friend, I own one and a half per cent,' so that was quite an eye-opener for him.

Things began to get difficult on the Clyde in the 1960s and there was the Fairfield Experiment and Upper Clyde Shipbuilders. I was never one of those who was hostile to the Fairfield Experiment but one thing is absolutely clear, they proved nothing. In large part of course, that was because it was swept up into UCS as a consequence of the Geddes Report. We didn't like the Geddes Report at all. I knew Reay Geddes and he was kind enough to say to me that I wasn't going to like the report so I had better come for a chat. So I went and had a chat the day after the report came out and I told him that it wasn't going to work. They were putting three loss-making firms in with two, Connell's which was making ends meet and Yarrow's which was profitable into one firm which it was hoped would make a

profit. The loss makers were Stephen's, Brown's and Fairfield's and we were very much, as I've said, a public company and our shareholders simply wouldn't accept going into such an entity.

We went in eventually but in my view UCS was a disaster, you had profit makers flung in with loss makers, all companies had to come up to the wage level of the highest payer and all this did was to prop up the weak rather than supporting the strong. As John Davies, who was the Conservative Industry Minister at the time, asked, where should the money go and I said to him that it should go to the strong, don't prop up the lame ducks, you're pouring tax-payers money down the drain.

I don't know how Tony Hepper ended up as Chairman of UCS, he had no background or knowledge of shipbuilding. I won't say anything against him, but eventually he lost his job although that wasn't my fault. I can only assume that he was asked to be Chairman by the government of the day. The best business decision I ever made was getting out of UCS and I had a bottle of champagne on that day. We were lucky in that we had been able to do substantial modernisation. We acquired Blythswood and Barclay Curle which gave us the space and scope to modernise while still building and in that sense we were fortunate it allowed us to do the covered berth and make other improvements.

I can't see the shipbuilding industry picking up, you can't stop yards being built abroad and that's one of the reasons for the state of the industry. Everyone wants their own shipbuilding industry whether it's economic or not. Modernisation was too slow in this country and the trade unions were also too slow in modernising their working practices, so there were faults on both sides, both had a part to play. I feel very depressed looking at the river now. In the old days we used to go 'doon the water' as they say, and you'd pass yard after yard. I couldn't go down the river now, it is all too sad.

COLLAPSE

World War I dealt shipbuilding and marine engineering in Britain and on the Clyde a blow from which it never recovered. In its requirement to build warships for the national emergency, merchant shipbuilding fell to virtually nothing during hostilities. Trade connections had been eroded, goodwill lost and over vast swathes of the oceans, foreign shipping lines had captured routes and trade formerly the preserve of the British. Competition in shipbuilding, which had been relatively insignificant before the war, became serious with Denmark, Holland, Italy, Japan, Sweden, the United States, and later, Germany all becoming major players.

The postwar boom of 1919 and 1920 masked this underlying trend. On the Clyde, Fairfield had a larger order book than at any time in the previous years. John Brown's had work under way on all of its berths which was 'a condition of matters which has never existed before in the history of the yard'. At Greenock, Scott's had booked seventeen merchant orders by 1920. The boom was sustained by the fact that shipowners were prepared to pay almost any price for ships to share in the expected boom. This boom evaporated in 1920 and turned quickly into a slump. As Colonel Denny of Dumbarton put it at a launch in December, 'six or eight months ago a ship was not to be had except at a ransom price'. The fall in prices, however, would mean that 'trades would suffer somewhat severely'.

Suspension and cancellation of contracts duly followed. Worse was to come when in 1921 the British government signed the Washington Naval Treaty which placed limits on warship construction thereby denying, what for many yards, had been a major source of employment.

The impact was immediate. Following the 1919 strike by which a shorter working week and continuation of the wartime bonuses were gained, industrial power swung back in favour of the employers. Wages were forced down and unemployment rose. Average weekly wages in John Brown's, for example, fell from 41s11d (£2.10) in 1920 to 28s4d (£1.42) in 1923, and the average number of men at work in the yard per week fell from over 9,000 in 1920 to under 3,500 in 1923. Unemployment in Scottish shipbuilding, which had been two per cent in 1920 had reached nearly 40 per cent by 1923. Thus, added to an already bitter and ingrained system of industrial relations, were the grim memories of unemployment and family hardship.

Those in charge of the industry were no longer the inventors, innovators and visionaries of yesteryear. Even as late as 1945, of the twenty four shipyards and eighteen marine establishments that remained on the Clyde, well over half were still owned by the descendants of the founding fathers: Scott's, Lithgow's, Stephen's and Yarrow's, to name but a few. The thrust, however, had gone. The Clyde had long basked in the sunshine as the world's pre-eminent shipbuilding centre and in the resonance of 'Clyde Built'. Attitudes, where they were not ones of overweening superiority, were now utterly defensive. For example, Sir James Lithgow could assert that as technical equipment, organising capacity, naval architecture and the craftsmanship of individual shipyard workers were concerned, 'this country has nothing to fear in comparison with either Germany or any other country'. The problem, according to Sir James, was that 'our lower hours and higher wages' had burdened British shipbuilding, 'with a much greater cost than our world competitors'. The sole problem, therefore, was labour.

Such views would form the basis of a twenty year trope from Lithgow. A management style and organisation of work which had served the industry well in the nineteenth century during the revolutions of wood to iron and sail to steam – the aloof uniform of the bowler hat and the strict craft-based methods of work – were fast becoming redundant. Heavily wedded to a product base defined by the late nineteenth century order book and steam as a form of propulsion, the industry's lack of innovation, or even response to innovation elsewhere, became a

Looking over the berths at Govan Shipbuilders in 1978 (Photo courtesy of Stuart Lindsay)

serious problem in the twentieth century. New products – the tanker; the container ship; the diesel; welding – and new yard layouts to take advantage of new technology, were often scorned. If they were indulged, it was in the battleground of an intractable industrial relations system with both capital and labour fighting to control the work process.

In a situation of endemic job insecurity, labour was unlikely to acquiesce in the introduction of technology which would deny or de-skill jobs. Management too, long used to a system where the casual nature of labour could be used to vary costs, was not keen to incur the costs of fixed capital investment. Such attitudes would persist long after they had outlived their rationale or even, at one point, their apparent usefulness.

Despite periodic glimmers of revival, the slump continued throughout the 1920s and was then exacerbated by the international economic depression in the 1930s. The situation was symbolised by the suspension of work on the giant Cunarder, No. 534, the ship which would become the *Queen Mary* at John Brown's. Employment at the Clydebank yard fell to an average of 422 per week in 1932 and registered unemployment in Scottish shipbuilding reached nearly 70 per cent. Schemes of self-help inevitably concentrated on reducing capacity. The body which carried out this rationalisation was National Shipbuilders Security Ltd, chaired by Sir James Lithgow. Its first victim was the giant Dalmuir yard of William Beardmore which was purchased and dismantled.

The implications were clear – if one of the most modern yards in the country, having invested heavily with an eye to new products and markets, could not survive then who could?

Between 1931 and 1937 NSS closed yards on the Clyde at Ardrossan, Old Kilpatrick, Dumbarton, Scotstoun, Paisley, Port Glasgow, Irvine, Govan, Glasgow and Greenock.

It was warship building which pulled the industry out of crisis. The rearmament programmes of 1933-4 to 1938-9 made provision for some 754,000 tons on new construction. Between 1934 and 1939 eleven Clyde firms were sharing sixty six Admiralty contracts between them, with the lion's share going to Fairfield, John Brown, Scott, Stephen, Denny and Yarrow.

Rearmament may well have restored profitability but few expected that it would last beyond the end of the programme. One of the lessons of the interwar period, at least as far as the owners were concerned, was that the restoration of liquidity, rather than investment in the future, was the key to short-term survival. Indeed short-termism had become ingrained, and militated against the industry taking advantage of the conditions which the post-1945 market would offer. For owners and managers the abiding lesson of the disastrous interwar period may well have been that ambitious schemes of capital investment would not work and that any increase in capacity would be the short road to ruin.

For labour, the effect of the interwar years had been appalling. The wage cuts, the rates of unemployment and the scale of deprivation burned deep into the consciousness. The current and future generations of workers could hardly avoid this conditioning and anything that even appeared to threaten job security would be resisted. In truth, the past was a prison from which neither the Clyde nor the rest of British shipbuilding could escape.

If shipbuilders had been unprepared for the interwar slump so too were they unprepared for the post-1945 boom. Foreign competition now became deadly serious and world shipbuilding output expanded from 1.2 million gross registered tons (grt) in 1947 to 9.3 million grt in 1958. British output scarcely grew at all however, increasing from 1.2 million to 1.4 million grt. The output of the Clyde did increase from 375,000 grt in 1947 to 417,000 grt in 1958 but both the Clyde and British shipbuilding posted their record post-war launchings in the same year, 1955, at 1.47 million grt and 485,000 grt respectively.

Employment in the industry had not, however, recovered. On the Clyde there were 58,000 directly employed in shipbuilding in 1951, lower than the 67,000 of 1931 and a far cry from the near 100,000 employed in the West of Scotland in 1921. Across the trades, the job opportunities presented in the postwar market outside shipbuilding, whether in terms of pay, conditions or security of employment, were too much and they voted with their feet.

Throughout the 1947-1958 period the Clyde averaged just over 30 per cent of UK launches, but given that UK shipbuilding represented an ever declining share of world launches there was little comfort in this. By 1956 Japan had taken over as the world's leading shipbuilding nation and in 1958, West Germany pushed Britain, who now held just over 15 per cent of world launchings, into third place.

The staple products of Clyde and UK shipbuilding – the liner, cargo-liner, cross-channel ferries, dredgers and the tramp – were all types in trend decline. The strategic decline of the Royal Navy resulted in fewer warships with a consequent reduction in naval orders and in warship building yards. Many of the developments in specialist ship technology, most notably the container ship, were simply ignored. True, many yards built tankers, indeed the Blythswood made them a speciality, but many owners considered them an intrusion into the normal order book which gave no employment to the outfitting trades. The motor ship eclipsed the steam propelled ship resulting in the majority of Clyde builders having to build on licence. Although welding had been widely adopted it was only at the expense of widespread overmanning which tended to negate the economic and productivity gains which the new technology bestowed. Few yards took advantage of new layouts and 'flow-line' production techniques which German, Swedish and Japanese yards adopted with gusto. With reasonable profits still being made employing largely traditional methods, there was

little incentive and such modernisation as was attempted was haphazard and piecemeal.

Still, all these conditions were masked until the onset of the mild recession of 1958-1961 which served to confirm the fear that the long expected postwar slump, on the post World War I model, had at last arrived. The Clyde launched its lowest volume of merchant ships, 333,000 grt, in 1961, since 1939, and its percentage share of UK output fell below 30 per cent for the first time in the post-1945 period. The workforce in shipbuilding in the West of Scotland was now down to 47,000 people.

As profits were squeezed, some shipbuilders and marine engineers decided that closure was preferable to a repeat of the interwar years. Between 1962 and 1964, Denny, Blythswood, A&J Inglis, Harland & Wolff, Simon & Lobnitz, Hamilton and the Ardrossan Dockyard had closed, many taking their engine works with them. None of the closures occasioned either surprise or distress; they were, in the main, voluntary, and the river and economy in general were vibrant enough to absorb the resultant unemployment with comparative ease.

What did occasion shock, however, was the spectacular failure, in 1965, of Fairfield. The yard employed 3,000 people, had spent heavily on modernisation and had an order book worth £32 million. This was not voluntary liquidation but bankruptcy and a grim portent of things to come. Given that the Labour Government had mounted a full-scale enquiry into the shipbuilding industry – the subsequent conclusions being known as the Geddes Report – it was decided to facilitate an ambitious rescue of Fairfield's as a 'proving ground' for new methods in shipbuilding. The 'Fairfield Experiment', as it was known, was bitterly resented by other Clyde shipbuilders who detested the idea that non-shipbuilders could run a shipbuilding yard. Embroiled in near permanent controversy, the 'experiment' never ran its full course, being swept up into

Men of the Sheet Iron Shop at Fairfield in 1962

Upper Clyde Shipbuilders with its management team dispersed and its ideas emasculated. Perhaps, but only perhaps, a chance had been missed to break the vicious circle of poor productivity, relatively high prices, late delivery dates and poisonous industrial relations.

The outcome of the Geddes inquiry into shipbuilding was that the yards should be grouped around river centres. On the Clyde two groups were formed: Upper Clyde Shipbuilders, comprising Fairfield, Connell, Stephen, Yarrow and John Brown; and, on the Lower Clyde, Scott and Lithgow merged to become Scott Lithgow. Neither was a success.

In June 1971, Upper Clyde Shipbuilders collapsed. Despite the massive profile and the dignity engendered by the subsequent work-in, the hard facts were that the level of total liabilities over assets in 1971 stood at more than £28 million. In four short years the company had consumed over £65 million in public money, the vast majority of which had been consumed in meeting losses and in working capital. The high profile of the work-in did, however, force the government into an infamous U-turn. Clydebank was saved for oilrig production, the warship yard Yarrow was returned to the private sector and the former Fairfield yard, now reconstituted as Govan Shipbuilders, became the focus of reconstruction but primarily for 'social reasons'. Stephen's, which had been retained as a fabrication facility only, closed. Connell's was reconstituted as Scotstoun Marine and survived until 1980 while Barclay Curle, arguably the most modern of all the Clyde yards, was closed by its owners Swan Hunter in 1967.

The massive well-spring of support for the UCS work-in was testimony to the fact that the industry still resonated in the public consciousness.

It is difficult, though, to resist the conclusion that UCS acted with remarkable cackhandedness in the market place. The very public row over the breakdown of the QE2 on trials allowed the press an unfair field day attacking the very concept of 'Clyde-built'. British shipbuilding in 1972 produced only 4.6 per cent of world output and the Clyde was producing less than 20 per cent of UK output. The industry was on its way to statistical irrelevance.

The Scott Lithgow merger faired little better than UCS. The merger was originally predicated on the company moving into the Very and Ultra Large Crude Carrier market. Such a strategy, however, was ruined by the Arab-Israeli War in 1973 and subsequent hike of 400 per cent in oil prices. World shipbuilding collapsed, with output falling from 36 million grt in 1975 to just over 600,000 grt in 1979. On the Clyde output fell from 283,000 grt to 86,000 grt, just over 14 per cent of UK output. Employment in shipbuilding in the West of Scotland was down to 29,000. With state money pouring in (and out) of the industry, it was nationalised in 1977. As The Economist noted, 'public ownership was now the last hope of the industry if it was to survive'.

But, by 1980, Scott Lithgow had posted a loss of over £42 million, over a third of British Shipbuilders losses, and a combination of gaps in the order book, high inflation, low productivity, late deliveries and lack of naval demand all contributed to a deteriorating position. Accordingly, Scott Lithgow was placed in the newly created Offshore Division of British Shipbuilders to take advantage of the burgeoning market in oilrigs. Despite winning orders, this proved to be a disaster. On two big contracts, Scott Lithgow ran up losses of nearly £17 million. Clearly exasperated with the situation, the Chairman of British Shipbuilders, Sir Robert Atkinson, declared that the yard had, '5,000 deaf men, a history of losses and late deliveries, high absenteeism and poor industrial relations'. Given that Scott Lithgow threatened to bring down the whole structure of British Shipbuilders, it was privatised in 1984, being sold off to Trafalgar House. It was placed on a care

Lunch time outside Govan Shipbuilders in the 1980s

and maintenance basis in 1988 and closed in 1990. Shipbuilding, which had once dominated the waterfront from Newark to Greenock had all but disappeared as a major employer of labour and over 9,000 jobs had been lost directly. Marine engine building which had heralded the start of shipbuilding in the early 1800s had ceased altogether.

The privatisation of the shipbuilding industry under Mrs Thatcher's government was, as with so much of manufacturing industry, little more than a gigantic con trick to reduce capacity. In a dubious deal the Norwegian company Kværner, acquired Govan, Clark Kincaid and Ferguson. At the same time, GEC acquired Yarrow. In 1999, Kværner pulled out of shipbuilding and BAe Systems acquired Yarrow and later Govan.

By the year 2000, shipbuilding yards on the Clyde comprised, Govan, Yarrow and Ferguson at Newark. Depressingly, the Ailsa yard at Troon announced its closure that year.

The former John Brown shipyard, once world famous for luxury passenger ships, remains hopeful of winning some oil related work. Paradoxically, the world demand for luxury cruise ships has never been higher.

A once great industry had become little more than a rump employing a few thousand people. Banks, call centres and other commercial ventures are now all more important sources of employment than shipbuilding. This rapid decline was occasioned by the intransigence of management and labour which simply could not adjust to the new markets and production systems of the twentieth century.

Whatever the truth, by 2000 the Clyde was a quiet river. Its former rationale had ceased to exist, the great industrial age was past, probably forever. The industrial waterfronts are now shopping centres or the clichéd 'prestigious luxury housing developments'. What had once sustained thousands of workers had changed, by the start of the new century, into little more than post industrial landscape. In the words of Yeats, 'all was changed, changed utterly'.